But
I Tell
You

BUT I TELL YOU receives praise:

L.L. Barkat
author of Stone Crossings: Finding Grace in Hard and Hidden Places *(InterVarsity Press, spring 2008)*

> Reading *But I Tell You* is like sipping jasmine tea on a peaceful morning. It is quiet and approachable, sweetly preparing us to meet the day. But watch out: Oberst's book, like its subject the Sermon on the Mount, has a flavor of challenge we cannot easily put aside.

Tim Burdick
editor of simpleriver.org and student at George Fox Evangelical Seminary

> The Sermon on the Mount has always been a difficult passage to realize today, and one that is often brushed over as a utopian dream. Oberst reaches back to the ancient texts, however, and brings out a core modern-day relevance that is both challenging and practical. *But I Tell You* is a great book for anyone who wants to spend a week or an entire year reading through the heart of what Jesus taught.

Robert A. Crandall
pastor and educator

> *But I Tell You* is a fresh and refreshing look at the Sermon on the Mount in bite-sized chapters. It is not some self-improvement "fluff," but solid spiritual meat. The writing is clear, cogent, and compelling, making it easier to digest. But a warning: It is also convicting!
>
> This attractive paperback is an excellent resource for personal study, reflection, and spiritual growth. Small groups would do well to use it for study and discussion. And teachers and leaders in the church will find excellent material for their ministries. The use and explanation of the Greek gives added support and authority.
>
> My hope is that others are as challenged and encouraged by this book as I have been.

Faith Marsalli
pastor, Klamath Falls (Oregon) Friends Church

> Karen's book offers its reader a challenging and practical view of the most radical sermon Jesus ever preached. This Greek scholar makes the original language accessible to us all. Her fresh perspective on the Sermon on the Mount inspires one to move from complacency to action.

David L. McKenna
educator, administrator, author

> The Sermon on the Mount is like a diamond in the light. With each turn of the gem, a new facet of truth shines through. Karen L. Oberst gives us that kind of insight as she makes key words from the Greek text come alive with creative meaning and practical application. *But I Tell You* is a resource for daily reading, with a point to ponder as we go on our way.

Arthur O. Roberts
professor at large, George Fox University, Newberg, Oregon

> Karen L. Oberst writes lucidly and with refreshing insights about a familiar portion of Jesus' teachings: the Sermon on the Mount. Her knowledge of original languages is matched by a good grasp of contemporary verbal culture. This enables her to convey in a conversational mode both the implications and the applications of these important New Testament teachings. The book thus offers thoughtful Christian readers a unique blend of authentic text and creative paraphrase.

Walter Wink
author; professor emeritus of biblical interpretation,
Auburn Theological Seminary, New York

> The Sermon on the Mount is the most radical statement of Jesus' new reality, and *But I Tell You* is a good place to engage its challenge to a new life. This lively and readable book is made the more valuable thanks to the author's knowledge of Greek. Read, and enjoy.

But I Tell You

JESUS INTRODUCES A BETTER WAY TO LIVE

Karen L. Oberst

BARCLAY PRESS
Newberg, Oregon

BUT I TELL YOU
Jesus Introduces a Better Way to Live

© 2007 by Karen L. Oberst

Published by Barclay Press
211 N. Meridian St., #101, Newberg, OR 97132
www.barclaypress.com

ISBN 978-1-59498-010-7

All rights reserved.
No part of this publication may be reproduced,
stored in a retrieval system, or transmitted in
any form or by any means—for example, electronic,
photocopy, recording—without the prior
written permission of the publisher.
The only exception is brief quotations
in printed reviews.

All Scripture quotations, unless otherwise indicated, are taken from the *Holy Bible, New International Version®. NIV®.* Copyright © 1973, 1978, 1984 by International Bible Society. Used by permission of Zondervan. All rights reserved.

Some Scripture quotations from *The Message.* Copyright © by Eugene H. Peterson 1993, 1994, 1995, 1996, 2000, 2001, 2002. Used by permission of NavPress Publishing Group.

DEDICATION

In memory of Bonnie Clark,
who would have been thrilled to see this.

ACKNOWLEDGMENTS

Thanks to all who looked at
But I Tell You: Jesus Introduces a Better Way to Live
in the manuscript stage and gave suggestions
and encouragement. At the risk of
leaving people out, particular thanks to
Laurel Ann Strieby, always my first reader;
to Faith Marsalli; and to Marye Hefty.

Thanks also to my editor Lisa Delzer Cox,
who made the book much better than it was.

Finally, a big thanks to Mark O'Neill,
who drew the "humility" comic strip
especially for this book.

CONTENTS

introduction — A Change in Perspective ❖ 1

1 **The Internal Beatitudes** ❖ 5
Entrance into the Kingdom
God Our Advocate
Recognizing Your True Worth

2 **The External Beatitudes, part 1 — Attitude** ❖ 17
Justice for All
A Better Way
Eyewitnesses

3 **The External Beatitudes, part 2 — Action** ❖ 27
Bringing Reconciliation
The Results of Action, part 1
The Results of Action, part 2

4 **Salt and Light** ❖ 39
Salty Christians
God's City Blazes with Light
Christian Lamps
Making it Personal

5 **Everything Old is New Again** ❖ 49
Jesus as the Fulfillment of Prophecy
God's Words Last
A Warning to Teachers
Inward and Outward Righteousness

6 **The First Law — Murder & Anger** ❖ 59
(Sins of the Mind)
Don't let Your Anger Get the Better of You
Take the Initiative to Make Things Right with Your Friends
Take the Initiative to Make Things Right with Your Enemies

7 **The Second and Third Laws—The Marriage Vow ❖ 69 (Sins of the Senses)**
   Don't Get Carried Away by Your Desire
   Drastic Problems Require Drastic Remedies
   Divorce

8 **The Fourth Law—Integrity ❖ 79**
   I Do Solemnly Swear
   Impertinence, Cheek, Chutzpah, and Other Forms of Irreverence

9 **The Fifth Law—Creative Nonviolence ❖ 87 (Jesus' Third Way)**
   An Eye for an Eye: The Old Testament Standard
   The Infamous "Turn the Other Cheek"
   Exposing an Unmerciful System
   Going the Extra Mile
   Living Generously

10 **The Sixth Law—Love Your Enemies ❖ 101**
   The Old Law
   The New Law—Love Your Enemies
   Of Sun and Rain
   God Doesn't Grade on the Curve
   Grow Up!

11 **Reaching Out To Others ❖ 115**
   Who Are You Trying to Impress?
   "I'm Not Really a Kingdom Subject; I Just Play One on the Stage"
   Stealth Giving

12 **Teaching On Prayer ❖ 125**
   Praying to the Audience
   Simple, Honest Prayer
   The Lord's Prayer
   More Words on Forgiveness

13 **Teaching on Fasting ❖ 143**
   High Tragedy

14 **Teaching on Things** ❖ 147
   Where Is Our Treasure?
   Keep Your Glass Clean
   One Boss

15 **Teaching on Trust** ❖ 157
   Consider the Wild Birds
   Consider the Wildflowers
   Stop Your Worrying!
   Seek the Kingdom

16 **A Reminder about Relating to Others** ❖ 169
   Avoiding Judgment
   Of Sawdust and Roof Beams
   Dogs, Pigs, and Pearls

17 **Giving as God Gives** ❖ 179
   Ask, Seek, Knock
   Giving Good Gifts
   The Golden Rule

18 **Living Alertly** ❖ 189
   Know Your Gates
   Of Prophets, Trees, and Fruit
   Is Your Name on the Roll?

19 **A Final Story & The Reaction of the Crowd** ❖ 201
   A Building Lesson from the Carpenter
   Astonishment at the Unique Teaching

Expanded Translation ❖ 209

Notes ❖ 223

For Further Reading ❖ 227

introduction

A CHANGE IN PERSPECTIVE

I remember my first pair of glasses. I was only nine years old, but I still recall the wonder of being able to make out every leaf on a tree. I was amazed at what a difference two small pieces of glass made in my perception of the world.

In a Chinese folktale called "The Neighbor's Shifty Son," a farmer's ax disappears. Believing his neighbor's son to have stolen it, the farmer keeps watch all day, noticing how guilty both his neighbor and his neighbor's son appear. On the following day, however, he finds his ax in the field where he left it. When he next looks at his neighbor, he sees a perfectly normal person with his perfectly innocent son. Learning the truth changed the way he saw his neighbor.

Changes in perspective happen to all of us on a greater or lesser scale. Buying glasses; discovering a previously unknown fact; reading a book; hearing a poignant question, a conversation, or a Scripture passage at the right time can change our outlook. Someone may say, "Try to see the situation from my point of view," and, if we are willing, we realize truths we never thought of before.

The biblical passage of Matthew chapters 5—7, also known as the Sermon on the Mount, involves God offering just such a change in perspective as Jesus talks about who we are as citizens of God's kingdom and about our attitudes toward God and toward others.

Before I started studying this passage I thought of it as a collection of Jesus' teachings randomly stuck together. In actuality nothing could be further from the truth. I had been used to Paul's rough-and-ready style, Greek coming from a man so brimming over with his message that he seems to have dashed the words on paper. In contrast, Matthew is elegant and scholarly, with beautifully crafted sentences. Having learned many of these verses in the King James Version as a child, I was surprised by words I had always taken for granted but in which I suddenly discovered new meaning.

Was the sermon a single talk given by Jesus to a specific group on a specific day, or a distillation of his teachings gathered together in one place? Either way, this is concentrated kingdom instruction—a seminar in life given by the Author and Creator. It is heady, perspective-changing stuff, guaranteed.

I am not a theologian by training or profession. I was a Greek major at Houghton College in Houghton, New York, and have relied heavily on lexicons—one for koine Greek, the Greek of Jesus' era, and another for classical Greek—for translation. Rather than reading commentaries and other books on the sermon, I have tried to follow the Greek where it leads, supplemented by research on customs of the times. My prayer is that God will use these words to awaken in others some of the awe and life-changing revelations I have found and that God will speak and move through this little book.

About Language

The Greek language, unlike English, contains separate words for the plural *you*, used when speaking to a group, and the singular *you*, used when speaking to a single person. In an attempt to overcome this English deficiency, I have inserted the clarifications of *[pl.]* and *[sing.]*, respectively, where I felt it would enhance understanding of the text.

The translations at the beginning of chapters and sections are a literal translation of the Greek, following the order of the words in Greek, and so may sound strange in English. These literal translations will help those who would like to match up the Greek of the original text with its English meaning.

I have tried to avoid sexist reference as much as possible. Instead, I have chosen *child* instead of *son*, and *heavenly Parent* rather than *heavenly Father*, consistent with biblical teaching that God is both male and female. Whatever the take on this sensitive issue, I hope my choice of language won't detract from the wonder and richness of the sermon.

Expanded Translations

I have taken the verse or verses discussed in each section and provided a translation. These translations are not literal, but rather represent what the Greek implies. For those who would like to see these together, I have compiled them at the end of the book.

Verses from other places in the Bible are from the New International Version (NIV), except where noted.

Introduction to Matthew 5

The verses of Matthew 5 are often called the "Beatitudes," harkening back to the Latin Vulgate in which each verse begins with the word *breati*, meaning "blessed."

Though the original Greek was not divided into chapters and verses, the assigned chapter divisions here split the sermon nicely. The beginning of Matthew 5 serves as an introduction to the Sermon on the Mount; in an executive summary, the Beatitudes begin by telling us how to get into the kingdom of God and also how kingdom citizens behave. Jesus then presents the same concepts differently, using metaphors to show how kingdom citizens interact with others. The chapter ends with a series of contrasts—not to distinguish between the old law and the new, but rather between false interpretations of the law and the law's true meaning.

One of the two themes becomes clear right away: the contrast Jesus makes between attitude and action. The Beatitudes begin by addressing attitude (blessed are the poor in spirit) and moving outward to appropriate action (blessed are the peacemakers). A right attitude is the first step into a kingdom lifestyle, but attitude without action gets you nowhere. On the other hand, action without the right attitude of the heart leads to hypocrisy and insincerity, a problem discussed further in Matthew 6. The other dominant theme of Matthew 5 is respect, a topic addressed later in verses about the law.

Blessed Be...

There is no gentle introduction to the sermon. Jesus doesn't ease his listeners into new ways of thinking. He doesn't begin with a disclaimer or by hedging his words to soften reality. Instead he turns things upside down. While we usually think of the rich and successful as being blessed by God, Christ begins with the shocking announcement, "Blessed are the destitute in spirit."

The word usually translated "blessed" is *makarios* in Greek. This is a poetic form of the word *makar*, which originally referred to the bliss of the gods, a euphoria that could not be known by mere mortals. In Jesus' time the longer word had come to mean blessed, fortunate, happy, and privileged. It is the word that might be used to describe someone who just won the lottery; is pulled out alive from the rubble of a building days after searchers have given up looking for anyone; or finds out Grandma's old pot is worth millions. In short, *makar* is for someone who has had luck beyond the expected and is absolutely thrilled.

In the sermon, Jesus invites us to change our perspective on whom we see as *makarios* and instead look at whom God considers lucky, blessed, fortunate, happy, or privileged.

1

αβγδεζηθικλμνξοπρςστυφχψωαβγδεζηθικλμνξοπρςστυφχψωαβγδεζηθικλμνξοπρςστυφχψω

THE INTERNAL BEATITUDES

Outsider

by Karen L. Oberst

Beggar, that's what I am.
Hand out, asking.
Always needing. Always wanting.
Found me a sweet place, though.
Kind man. Kind. Soft. A little crazy maybe.
Gives me food. Gives me clothes, and a place to sleep.
I got it made. All I gotta do is ask—sometimes not even that.
Got it made. Got it made.

Looked in the man's house today.
Pretty place, but not so full of stuff as I thought.
Kind man's not rich—or maybe not showy.
Got him a big family too. Nice clothes. Good food.
And happy. And...more than happy.
They all have the same look he has.
The look he called "love."
Maybe I ain't got it made yet. Maybe not yet.

"Mister, mister, please I want..."
"To come inside? Do. Come enjoy the love."
"Oh yes, I....What's the catch? Always a catch."

"You'll become part of my family: loved and loving.
You'll learn to give. Learn to see and to help, and to care
About me, and my family, and these outsiders. I'll help you."
I look at the beggars—hands out, wanting, pleading—love them?
Do I really want in that much? Do I?

μακάριοι οἱ πτωχοὶ τῷ πνεύματι
ὅτι αὐτῶν ἐστιν ἡ βασιλεία τῶν οὐρανῶν

Blessed are the destitute in spirit,
for of them is the kingdom of heaven.

Matthew 5:3 · Entrance into the Kingdom

Attitude Matters

If the Sermon on the Mount tells us the characteristics of the citizens of God's kingdom, Matthew 5:3 tells us how to become part of that kingdom. We must first recognize that we have nothing that can gain us admittance—not wealth, power, prestige, nor any earthly connections. Nor can sacrificing, serving on committees, maintaining perfect church attendance, tithing, evangelizing, teaching Sunday school, going to the mission field, preaching, living a moral life, marching for peace, or even being martyred for our testimony. Although these are admirable, we must remember that though our actions should grow out of our faith they are not a substitute for it. Nor do they gain us points with God.

The story of the lost son in Luke 15 shows us an example of this. The younger son of a wealthy landowner asks for his inheritance immediately, and taking the money, heads off to the big city. Unfortunately, when he runs out of money he also runs out of friends and when a famine hits the town, the only work he can find is slopping pigs—not at all a nice job for a kosher Jewish boy. Eventually he comes to his senses, realizing that the hired hands on his father's estate are better off than he. So he starts home, determining to ask his father to take him on as one of the help. When his father spies him walking up the road, he runs out, welcomes his lost son back to the family, and decrees a great feast to celebrate. This entire time the older son had faithfully stayed home, worked hard, and kept the rules. But upon his younger brother's return and his father's accepting welcome, anger and pride dominate the older son's heart and he is left out in the cold—by choice—while everybody else celebrates his brother's homecoming.

So it is with us. As long as we serve for others to notice, we have missed the boat and the party. We don't earn our way into the family through service and hard work. Jesus welcomes us despite our foolishness, and all we have to do is accept that great gift in humble thankfulness.

The older brother's attitude—sulking outside and feeling sorry for himself—is one with which we can all identify. At the same time, we must come to understand that the attitude of the kingdom is not who worked the hardest, but rather, who is part of the family when the celebrations begin.

The first step in getting into God's kingdom is realizing we have nothing for which to commend ourselves.

Being Poor

The word translated "poor" in this verse means being beggarly and wholly dependent on others for support. Where Luke 6:20 may be translated "Blessed are you who are destitute," Matthew adds "in spirit." With this, Matthew emphasizes the sermon he is recording is about attitude because our attitude commands our actions.

We have all experienced beggars either firsthand or via the media. We don't see people; we see hands out, looking for something free, sometimes bold and demanding, sometimes cringing and whining. I admit I don't like beggars. My first inclination is to tell them to get a job. Yet I know that isn't fair. True beggars—those who have little or no choice—can't get a job. In many places, a minimum-wage job will not begin to cover rent, food, health care, and other basic needs.

Beggars are those on the fringes of society who live in a culture but enjoy none of its benefits. In some ways they are worse off than slaves, who usually have food and shelter. Beggars take and don't give back because they have nothing. They are the disenfranchised, the ignored, and the outcast.

Once a month the church I attend has an unprogrammed service. We don't sing or have a sermon; instead, we wait and listen for what God will say to us and through us. I was shocked one morning when I received a vision of myself as a beggar outside God's door. It upset me terribly, even as I acknowledged the truth of the picture. Out of this vision came the poem at the beginning of this chapter. It wasn't until I began to study the sermon that I realized the vision wasn't the horrible thing it seemed, but rather the first step into kingdom life.

It is not easy to admit that we have nothing to offer God but our heart and ourself. We enter the kingdom as beggars—destitute, having nothing and knowing that we deserve nothing. Yet God sees us in the street, welcomes us in and calls us sons and daughters. We are changed from outcasts to heirs, from beggars to king's children. What amazing kindness! We are blessed indeed.

Expanded translation
> You are blessed when you realize you are no more than a beggar before God's door. The kingdom of heaven is made up of people just like you.

μακάριοι οἱ πενθοῦντες
ὅτι αὐτοὶ παρακληθήσονται

Blessed are those grieving,
for they will receive aid.

Matthew 5:4 · God Our Advocate

Good Grief

When I first looked at this verse, I saw what I expected to see—blessed are those who mourn, for they shall be comforted. I lost my best friend to cancer not long ago and my grief was deep, real, and lasting. I wanted that promise of comfort. But although God has given me peace, I no longer believe that kind of comfort is the sort meant here. The more I study the Beatitudes as a whole, the more I recognize that each piece builds on the one before.

The mourning described in Matthew 5:4 specifically refers to our spiritual condition. We realize in verse 3 that we are helpless to get into the kingdom of heaven ourselves and are totally without resources. Our response is deep sadness over our condition and mourning for our unworthiness. Harkening back to Luke 15, this is the realization of the younger son in a far country. He understood both that he yearned to go home and that he had no rights in that place of sanctuary.

Grief can be devastating and paralyzing, but grief can also be motivating. Only when the younger son hit bottom was he able to grasp what he had lost and find the impetus to head home. Grief grew into the hope and the prayer that he might at least become a servant in his father's house.

Our Advocate

The other key word in this verse is *paraklesontai*, which comes into English as *paraclete*, sometimes translated as "comforter" though usually as "advocate," or as we might say today, "defense attorney." We have come home helpless and broken, knowing we have no rights and deserve nothing but condemnation. What does God do? Far from condemning us or treating us as we deserve, our heavenly Parent steps forward, becomes our advocate, and welcomes us into the family.

Not only do we need comfort when we grieve, but restitution as well. Suppose the younger son had come home and been met by his father who simply said, "I love you, son. Don't let grief overwhelm you. It will be all right in time; you'll see." Without restitution to the family the son may have found a slightly better life than poverty, but it would have been cold comfort at best.

Like the landowner, our advocate restores us to our place in the family. Think of it! We come to the door of the kingdom as beggars, knowing that we have squandered everything and deserve nothing, and God not only invites us in but makes us heirs with all the rights and responsibilities that status entails. All we have to do is recognize our condition and ask for help. First John 1:9 reads, "If we confess our sins, he is faithful and just and will forgive us our sins and purify us from all unrighteousness." Confession isn't some mysterious process. The Greek word for "confession" simply means "agree." That is the door to the kingdom. We agree with God's assessment of our situation, and then God helps us.

Expanded translation

> Blessed are you who are brokenhearted when you realize how far you are from what you should be spiritually. God is your advocate and will take care of you.

μακάριοι οἱ πραεῖς
ὅτι αὐτοὶ κληρονομήσουσιν τὴν γῆν

Blessed are the meek,
for they shall inherit the land.

Matthew 5:5 · Recognizing Your True Worth

Just Who Do You Think You Are?

As we go through the sermon, we will find many transitional verses. This is the first. It is part of the theme of verses 3 and 4 in that it has to do with our relationship with God; it also goes with the verses following in that it refers to our relations with other people.

The usual connotations of the word *meek* are at best "humble" and at worst "downtrodden." We tend to think it means lying down and letting people walk all over us—not an attractive prospect! Yet the word does not mean that at all. The primary definition for *meek* is not being overly impressed by a sense of one's own self-importance.

Going back to Luke 15, we see an elder brother who is impressed by his own accomplishments. He believes that he is better than his brother and that his brother deserves less because he has achieved less and acted less responsibly. We must come to realize that we are nobody special—or rather, that all God's children are

This is from March 29, 2004; redrawn specifically for this book by Mark O'Neill in October 2006

BUT I TELL YOU

equally special. We are no better and no worse than anyone else regardless of our behavior.

This is a revolutionary point of view because if there's one thing humans are good at, it's finding reasons we are better than someone else.

"I would never cheat on my spouse like he/she does."

"Unlike Sue, I have never taken so much as a paper clip from the company."

"You know Joe has a little problem with drinking on the sly, don't you?"

"If I weighed as much as she does, I wouldn't eat that chocolate."

"Why doesn't he just get a job?"

"What can you expect—it's her upbringing."

"Those bleeding-heart liberals...."

"Those conservatives don't care about anyone but the rich...."

"What's wrong with him? Who does he think he is?"

One of the hardest things for us to grasp is that God doesn't have favorites. God doesn't care more for America than for any other nation. God doesn't care more for Christians than for non-Christians. God doesn't care more for the rich or the poor, the young or the old, men or women, black or white, sick or well, or any particular political point of view. God doesn't care more for the morally pure than for drug addicts, more for straight than for gay, more for victims than their oppressors.

We think we are right and have all the answers. But that's not the way it is in God's kingdom. There, we must listen and try to understand because we know we are all God's children. While we may choose to live separated from God's love and forgiveness, that doesn't mean God loves *us* any less. If God loves all children equally, then we need to begin acting like we are brothers and sisters and all children of the same heavenly Parent. When we remember we come to God as destitute beggars, we are less apt to judge our siblings, and when we can learn to act with respect instead of judgment, we learn to be humble and gentle.

God Always Loved You Best

There is another important side to humility, however. Some of us have no trouble valuing others above ourselves because we believe we have no value. Nothing could be further from the truth! At the same time God has no favorites, God favors us all.

A friend of mine, Jane, grew up in an abusive home. For her, verses like this one served only as a slam to a self-esteem already trodden into the ground. But one day Jane had an experience that changed her life: God told her, "I love you best." It was incredibly affirming and powerful for her to understand that God loved her exactly as she was and that she was important, even in her imperfection.

When we as human beings love somebody best, it means we love everybody else less. But God loves each of us best because God's love is absolute. Each of us is unique and created to fill our own place in God's kingdom. This place will remain empty if we don't fill it. If only we could learn to see others in this way; what a difference it would make in how we treat each other!

Heirs of the Promise

The last part of Matthew 5:5 always puzzled me. Are the meek supposed to inherit the new earth? What about those Christians who aren't particularly meek? Where will they be? And where does heaven fit into this?

When I took a closer look at the verse, I found the word usually translated as "earth" more commonly means "land." It is my belief that this is a New Testament restatement of the promise God gave to Abraham in Genesis 13:14-15: "The Lord said to Abram after Lot had parted from him, 'Lift up your eyes from where you are and look north and south, east and west. All the land that you see I will give to you and your offspring forever.'" In fact, Matthew 5:5 is a restatement of Psalm 37:9: "For evil men will be cut off, but those who hope in the Lord will inherit the land." It is God's promise to the chosen. Just as *shalom* became a shorthand word for "salvation"—that is, enjoying all the benefits that come with peace—

so *land* became shorthand for God's promise of an inheritance and God's assertion that things will work out in the end.

In Matthew 5:3, 5:4, and 5:5, we find the path to inheritance. First we realize we have nothing to offer from our own strength or goodness. We mourn for our failings, and find that God is ready to welcome us into the family. Finally, as a member of the family, we learn to see the world from a new perspective and realize that our heavenly Parent loves all humanity; that we are all equally children, brothers and sisters; and that we are all equally worthy of love. Once we have that lesson in our minds and hearts, we become true heirs of God's ancient promise to Abraham.

Expanded translation

> You are blessed when you come to understand your true worth—neither better than, nor less than anybody else. You have become one of the true inheritors of the promise of God to humanity, for by living this way, you show that you understand.

2

The External Beatitudes, part 1
ATTITUDE

μακάριοι οἱ πεινῶντες καὶ διψῶντες τὴν
δικαιοσύνην ὅτι αὐτοὶ χορτασθήσονται

Blessed are [the ones] hungering and thirsting [for]
righteousness, for they shall be satisfied.

Matthew 5:6 · Justice for All

Spiritual Hunger and Thirst

We now move into the Beatitudes that talk about our relations with others. In Matthew 5:5 we recognized that we are no better and no worse than anyone else. That leads to this verse, where we are filled with the desire to see our brothers and sisters treated fairly.

The words used here for "hungering" and "thirsting" are emphatic in the Greek. The first doesn't mean, "Oh, it's been four hours since breakfast; I guess I'll go eat lunch." Quite the contrary! The word for "hungering" means "famished." It is the same word used in Matthew 4:2, where Jesus had been in the wilderness for 40 days without food. Likewise, the word for "thirsty" doesn't mean "Oh sure, a glass of ice tea would be nice." It means "parched," and is the word used in John 19:28 when Jesus' lips are cracked and bleeding and he asks for liquid.

It is interesting how these words bracket Jesus' earthly ministry. He comes out of the desert famished, ready to begin his work, and ends on the cross, parched and dying. With these simple words we are not to think that justice is a nice idea, or agree in principle, or go along with our culture's standards. No! We are to seek justice as a person in the desert seeks an oasis—with life-and-death urgency.

The word often translated "righteousness" is *dikaiosuné*. It's a tricky word because it comes to us from a Greek society in which what was right was what was honorable, filtered through a Jewish society where what was right was what God commanded, to our own society where righteousness is an inward value. Inward righteousness needs to exist but it should not end there. Just as faith without works is dead, so righteousness that helps no one else serves no useful purpose. As Faith Marsalli said, "If your spirituality doesn't cause you to reach out, it's inauthentic."[1] Although we sometimes perceive it so, Christianity is not just an inward experience but an inward change that causes us to reach out to our brothers and sisters, especially those in need.

Dikaiosuné calls for behavior according to kingdom standards. We are to act as God would act toward our fellow human beings. This involves getting our life in order, getting right with God, and growing in Christian virtue. This new attitude also turns outward, wanting respect for all our brothers and sisters whether man or woman, black or white, or rich or poor. The Bible makes clear that God especially seeks justice for the poor and the powerless, and this is where our focus should be also.

Getting Practical

Is this easy? Definitely not. For myself, I'm still working on seeing alcoholics, drug addicts, oppressors, the violent, the arrogant—you name it—as my brothers and sisters. One of the reasons I appreciate riding the bus to work is that it exposes me to people I wouldn't be likely to meet otherwise. I've seen a woman drugged up to the point she didn't know where she was and wasn't able to control her body.

I've seen many people drunk. I've sat beside people who hadn't bathed in weeks and others just out of jail. I've listened to people talk about how their problems are never their own fault but instead the fault of either the "system" or someone in power who pays no attention. I've heard over and over how someone is going to get his or her act together and get off the streets, always soon. I've heard men talk casually about beating their girlfriends and about which are the most likely to grant them sexual favors. I've heard an abused teen talk about how the police took his stepfather to jail after a particularly violent episode. I've seen the long line each morning outside a restaurant that provides free breakfasts for the homeless. I've seen men who struggle with heroin addiction travel to the Veterans Affairs hospital to get their methadone. Each one believes he's going to kick the habit this time. I've heard the perpetual hope that if they just move to that town or this city, things will get better. I've heard bitterness, anger, disregard for life, and the frustrations of dealing with a system that doesn't care if they live or die.

These are our brothers and sisters. These are people who crave justice and fair treatment from a system where they get neither. These are the people to whom we are called to reach out, both as individuals and as a church. We are God's feet now in our world. We are God's hands in our world. When we see the world as God sees it and hear as God hears, then we should be moved to act as God would act. When we begin insisting on justice for this part of our family, Jesus says we will be satisfied.

Now that's a promise worth working for.

Expanded translation

> You are blessed when you are desperate to do right to others, to treat others fairly, and have a burning desire for justice, for you shall be satisfied in that desire.

μακάριοι οἱ ἐλεήμονες
ὅτι αὐτοὶ ἐλεηθήσονται

Blessed are the compassionate,
for they shall have compassion [shown to them].

Matthew 5:7 · A Better Way

Among the attributes of God, although they are all equal, mercy shines with even more brilliancy than justice. (Cervantes)

Being all fashioned of the self-same dust,
Let us be merciful as well as just. (Henry Wadsworth Longfellow)

Compassion is Better Than Justice

Pity, sympathy, mercy, and compassion—the Greek noun here can mean any of those things. What is the difference? Does it matter which word we choose?

> *Pity* is a feeling of sadness or pain aroused by the misfortune of others.
>
> *Sympathy* implies a feeling of kinship with the sufferer.
>
> *Mercy* is treating someone better than, or less severely than, they deserve. Where *pity* and *sympathy* may be only in the mind, *mercy* involves action.
>
> *Compassion* combines the tenderness of *pity*, the dignity of *sympathy*, and the active quality of *mercy*.[2]

In Matthew 5:6 we learned to ask for equal justice for all people. Here we learn the next step: reaching out in compassion to those in need. Justice is a challenge and our society is certainly nowhere near offering equal justice for all. It's easy to quote "justice for all" in America's Pledge of Allegiance and yet continue to think of people as a nameless mass.

We often feel pity for the hungry, the unemployed, or the homeless, and yet they remain faceless. We may have been brushed by troubles ourselves—being temporarily unemployed, having a loved one die, coming to a new place and being friendless for the moment—so that we feel sympathy for others in the same plight, without feeling compelled to do anything for them.

I'm a great supporter of causes. I have sponsored a child through a denominational program for years. I have given money to the Cousteau Society, the Salvation Army, Amnesty International, World Wildlife Fund, Habitat for Humanity, the Nature Conservancy, my *alma mater*, the Union of Concerned Scientists, local funds for the needy, foreign missions, the Red Cross, and innumerable others. It is easy. I write a check to various organizations once a year and feel like I am doing more than most people. It's amazing how easily we can fool ourselves, isn't it? I care about clear air and water, about saving disappearing species, about the hungry and the homeless, about responsible use of money and resources, and about war, but only enough to give money, never my time.

Matthew 5:7 calls us to give of ourselves and to reach out in compassion to our brothers and sisters. Unlike sitting down and writing a check, this can be quite difficult. I am strongly introverted and it's hard enough for me to reach out to my friends and family, let alone strangers. Because of this I'm starting small, trying to make helpfulness a way of life as I interact with my coworkers, my clients, and my friends. It is a small start, but a start nonetheless, and I pray it will grow.

Reaping What You Sow

Though reaching out in compassion is a good thing in and of itself, there is a selfish reason for doing so. When you show compassion to others, they will often show compassion to you. Jim Rohn, an inspirational business leader, says:

> How about this miracle...God says if you plant the seed, I will make the tree. Wow, you can't have a better arrangement than that. First, it gives God the tough end of the deal. What if you had to make a tree? That would keep you up late at night trying to figure out how to make a tree. God says, "No, leave the miracle part to me. I've got the seed, the soil, the sunshine, the rain and the seasons. I'm

God and all this miracle stuff is easy for me. I have reserved something very special for you and that is to plant the seed."[3]

This is encouraging news: It is our job to reach out, and it is God's job to take care of the results. God doesn't call us to success; God calls us to obedience. Anybody can be obedient—even me.

In Charles Dickens's *A Christmas Carol*, Ebenezer Scrooge, a successful yet ruthless businessman, is "as solitary as an oyster" with a shell built up to protect him from people. His life is consumed with money and there is no place left in his life for love or compassion for the less fortunate. One Christmas Eve, three spirits come to Scrooge. The first takes him to visit his past to remind him he wasn't always hard-hearted and distant. The second shows him the home of his secretary, Bob Crachit—a home where love coexists with poverty. But the true shock comes when the final spirit arrives and shows Scrooge his future. Scrooge sees himself on his deathbed; he hears no kind words spoken in his memory, no one expresses compassion on his passing. Even his nephew, who tried desperately to reach out to him, can find no good in the man. For the first time in many years, compassion awakens in Scrooge's heart with the true realization of the harsh life he has chosen. When he is given a second chance and realizes he is not, in fact, dead, but very much alive, he reaches out to meet the needs of Bob Crachit's family, to what family he has left, to the poor he has neglected for so long, and to God. Dickens calls it "the spirit of Christmas"; the Bible calls it compassion.

Let us move out and sow compassion not only for the sake of the hurting but for our own sake.

Expanded translation

You are blessed when you reach out to others in compassion, because in your turn you will receive compassion from others and from God when you are in need.

μακάριοι οἱ καθαροὶ τῇ καρδίᾳ
ὅτι αὐτοὶ τὸν θεὸν ὄψονται

Blessed are the clean [unalloyed] in heart,
because they God will see.

Matthew 5:8 · Eyewitnesses

We See What We Are

Asking ten friends to describe the same event often results in ten different tellings. Why? Perception depends on many different factors. Past experiences, how awake we are, what we had for breakfast, our last encounter, what we are reading, to whom we were speaking, whether we were paying close attention or daydreaming, whether an occurance was a surprise or something we expected to see, and how we feel about those involved all affect the way we see and remember. The list of influences is endless.

The Gospels are a good example of this. Some believe Matthew, Mark, Luke, and John aren't accurate because they don't agree word for word, but more likely their discrepancies are an indication of their authenticity. Different men heard, saw, and noted different things and remembered what was significant to them.

When we look at the world we see pieces, but not the whole. Kahlil Gibran admonishes, "Say not, 'I have found the truth,' but rather, 'I have found a truth.'"[4] In our postmodern world many believe that either all truths have equal value or actual truth does not exist. As Christians we believe we have found the ultimate truth, but we must remember our finiteness allows us to understand only part of this truth.

Think how our perceptions change as our heart changes. Sometimes this is sudden. When I was in college, a woman who lived on my dorm floor drove me crazy. Mary was loud whereas I was quiet. She pushed the rules and broke them as suited her purpose, whereas I was a good girl. She was generally disruptive and a difficult person with whom to live. Then one night I heard her read *The Giving Tree* by Shel Silverstein. The depth of feeling she put into that reading changed my view of her. For the first time I realized she was so much more than what I originally thought she was. We didn't become best friends, but as I began to understand her she became more than just someone to tolerate.

Other perceptual changes come more gradually. Studying the Bible and reading other books, my perception of truth has deepened over time. Doing my own digging through the Sermon on the Mount was a great joy, and over the course of writing this book, it has changed me in ways I never expected.

Eyewitnesses of God

This Beatitude also tells us what we must be to see the world as God sees it: clean in heart. What exactly does that mean? The word *katharos* in Greek has a variety of meanings. At its root and in that culture it means "ritualistically pure," like we associate with the word *kosher*. It can also mean "free from sin" or "morally responsible." Greek speakers saw the heart as the center of the will where moral decisions are made. We are to have wills made pure: focused on God and God alone. When that happens, we will see God in everything we do, everywhere we go, and in everyone we meet.

Robin Williams, a designer, calls *katharos* the Joshua Tree Principle.[5] Telling how she received a tree identification book that contained a picture of a Joshua tree, she was convinced she had never seen such a tree in her life. Yet the next time she walked around her neighborhood, she noticed that 80 percent of the homes had Joshua trees in their front yards. She never noticed the trees until a book brought them to her attention. The same thing can happen when we buy a new car—suddenly there are dozens of the same model on the road with us. What we are conscious of influences what we see. When our heart is tuned to God's heart, we see God.

Moving through these verses, we must first learn to seek justice for those who do not have it. Then we move from justice to mercy, reaching out to others in compassion. Finally, as we practice these things, we begin to see the world through God's eyes.

We know what God sees in this world: hurting people, helpless to assist themselves. God sees beloved children lost in poverty, hatred, guilt, and their own self-importance. God sees beloved children abusing each other, seeking power over one another and killing one other. God sees beloved children vilifying one another, turning one other into enemies and blaming one another. Are we prepared to see the world as God sees it? To see our society as God sees it? To see our brothers and sisters as God sees them? Quakers have a tradition of looking for that of God in everyone, or finding the divine spark that can be awakened in even the worst of us. When we look at the world with a pure heart attuned to God's heart, we will begin to see God before our eyes. What a frightening and exhilarating promise!

Expanded translation
> You are blessed when you view the world out of a heart like God's. You will begin to see God everywhere and in everyone you meet.

3

αβγδεζηθικλμνξοπρςστυφχψωαβγδεζηθικλμνξοπρςστυφχψωαβγδεζηθικλμνξοπρςστυφχψω

The External Beatitudes, part 2

ACTION

μακάριοι οἱ εἰρηνοποιοί
ὅτι αὐτοὶ υἱοὶ θεοῦ κληθήσονται

Blessed are the peacemakers,
because they children of God will be called.

Matthew 5:9 · Bringing Reconciliation

The peace witness along with the nonviolent struggle for justice is not some optional accessory in Christian living. It has to do with living out in frail human response an intimation of what Jesus lived out in going to his death for our salvation. (Dale Aukerman)

The Meanings of Peace

Who are the peacemakers? What does it mean to make peace? What does peace mean?

We tend to think of peace in one of two ways. The first is the large-scale view involving the absence of war. The United States is currently at peace with Canada; we are not at peace, as of this writing, with Iraq. The second is on a smaller, more personal scale involving peace and quiet. We think of peace as the absence of activity, noise, or demands. "The kids finally went to bed. Now maybe I'll get some peace!" This is not an unworthy definition. In our hectic, hurried, demanding lives, the rare moments of quiet are a real blessing. However, Jesus' definition of peace is all-encompassing.

The Greek word usually translated as "peace" has a broader meaning than we often give it. It refers to a state of harmony between both governments and individuals. Creating harmony takes more work than simply not fighting. I can create peace between myself and someone else by not talking to him or her—if we don't talk, we don't fight. This is how I handle politics at family gatherings. As the only Democrat in an extended family of Republicans, I keep peace by keeping my mouth shut. In this case, that's enough. An argument wouldn't change how either side thinks and I can still love them dearly, even though we choose differently at election time.

Important issues require more than silence and more than hope that if you ignore the situation it will go away. This attitude tends to be fatal in the workplace. I once had a boss who handled staff conflicts by talking first to one side and then to the other without ever allowing the two sides to come together to hash out differences. As a result, neither side ever learned to understand the other's point of view and hard feelings only grew harder.

In a different place where I worked, two employees from different areas had a disagreement. Another supervisor and I brought them together early on to talk *to* each other instead of *about* each other, and harmony was restored. This is one of the most basic ways of being a peacemaker.

Slightly different than the Greek concept of peace is the Hebrew word behind it, *shalom*. This is a complex word with many shades of meaning. At its simplest, *shalom* means the absence of war as the word *peace* does in English. However, this is only the beginning. Because Israel was an agrarian society where war meant disaster for crops and people but peace meant crops could grow and there would be trade, *shalom* came to have the broader meaning of prosperity. In *Keeping the Sabbath Wholly*, Marva Dawn says that *shalom* "begins in reconciliation with God and continues in reconciliation with our sisters and brothers—even our enemies. Moreover, *shalom* designates being at peace with ourselves, health, wealth, fulfillment, satisfaction, contentment, tranquility, and—to sum it all up—wholeness."[1]

Given the context, Matthew 5:9 talks about bringing harmony and reconciliation. As we have worked our way through the Beatitudes we have seen the move from recognizing we are equal in God's eyes, to asking for justice for our less fortunate brothers and sisters, to embracing the concept of mercy as a way of life until we have come to see the world as God sees it. We are now ready to do God's work in this world, bringing the good news of harmony and reconciliation between God and human beings and between one person and another—all the way up to nations reconciling with nations.

Peacemaking

Though all citizens of God's kingdom are called to be peacemakers, the process may look different for each person. As a boss you may be called to bring harmony to the workplace. As a mother or a teacher you may be called to teach the principles of cooperation to children. As a politician you may be called to bring together two or more sides of a dispute to find common ground and an acceptable compromise. You may feel called to go to a place of danger to help those on opposing sides learn to respect one another. Some professions are obviously peacemaking professions—counseling or mediating, for example—but we can all promote understanding in our own sphere of influence and curb those things that threaten it such as gossip, stereotyping, and deliberate misrepresentation. Seeking reconciliation also means letting go of revenge, grievances, and judgment. Though we may condemn actions, we must bring the word of love and reconciliation to our fellow human beings.

This also means governments need to be working much harder at finding peaceful solutions to conflict. I know I don't speak for all Christians when I say war is never right, but most of us agree that war is not good and should be avoided whenever possible. We must always remember that in war we are killing precious human beings, created by and loved by God. As this verse says, we show we are God's children when we are working for peace, harmony, and reconciliation.

Expanded translation

> You are blessed when you work to bring true harmony and reconciliation, for then you are acting as what you are—a child of God.

μακάριοι οἱ δεδιωγμένοι
ἕνεκεν δικαιοσύνης
ὅτι αὐτῶν ἐστιν ἡ βασιλεία τῶν οὐρανῶν

Blessed are the ones being harassed
because of righteousness,
because of them is the kingdom of heaven.

Matthew 5:10 · The Results of Action, part 1

Countercultural Thinking

I don't think this verse ever meant so much to me personally as it has since the tragic events of September 11, 2001. As the Quote Lady, I send out an inspirational quote each morning to several thousand people. After September 11, I deliberately chose a quote about forgiveness. It was a simple quotation: "Never does the human soul appear so strong as when it foregoes revenge, and dares to forgive an injury," by E. H. Chapin. This quote brought a spate of angry responses. Most were some variation of the idea that some things are unforgivable, but opinions were expressed strongly enough to make me feel vulnerable.

In the previous chapters we have talked about wanting justice for the poor and powerless. Citizens of the kingdom should also insist on justice for their enemies. We do not seek revenge but instead true justice that tries to understand all points of view. We are resident aliens here on earth struggling to hold the viewpoint of our true home with God.

In the 1960s we talked a lot about counterculture. The Sermon on the Mount is true countercultural living. It is 180 degrees from our success-oriented, in-your-face, bring-it-on, and if-you're-rich-enough-you-can-do-as-you-please attitudes. Instead, we must work to live morally pure lives in the midst of a culture that is anything but. We must be God-centered and not self-centered, which means we must look out for the people who have no power and no one to speak for them. We must bring people together and create harmony. We must not seek revenge, but instead cherish life as precious and seen by God as blessed.

Living out these values is bound to bring us into conflict with our society, no matter where we live.

Harassed for God's Sake

The word *dediogmeno,* often translated "persecuted," has an interesting background. It comes from a word that originally meant "to hunt," or, when used of a ship, "to drive before the wind." It is used in Philippians 3:13-14: "Forgetting what is behind, and straining toward what is ahead, I *press on* toward the goal to win the prize for which God has called me heavenward in Jesus Christ." *Dediogmeno,* then, does not always have a negative connotation. However, it also means harassing someone, especially because of his or her beliefs. I think of a pack of dogs after a deer, chasing it on and nipping at its heels.

Here, Jesus is talking about the petty comments that make us feel naïve or stupid and often wear us down.

"Come on, you can't tell me you believe in all that Bible stuff—no intelligent person really takes it seriously."

"Oh, don't be so naïve. People expect business to stretch the truth. It's part of the game."

"Loosen up and [fill in the blank]. You don't want the other guys [or girls] to think you're weird, do you?"

"If you're not 100 percent behind the president, you're unpatriotic."

We in the Western world probably won't be called on to lay down our lives for the truth or suffer some other major sacrifice, but little temptations plague us every day. This is where the rubber meets the road. When we are harassed for living out Sermon-on-the-Mount values, we know we are citizens of the kingdom. At the same time, it is important that we are only hassled for kingdom values—humility, justice, mercy, peacemaking—rather than for a holier-than-thou attitude that makes us difficult people with whom to live. People can be insulted for legitimate reasons.

It is certainly not fun to be laughed at and it's not easy to stand alone for something no one else values. Yet it's not those who live by the rules of the marketplace, the rules of politics, or the rules of this world who Jesus calls blessed. It is the one who stays true to Christ's teachings, who views the world as he does, and who lives according to kingdom standards.

At the height of the British Empire, Englishmen and women were found in all corners of the globe. But no matter where they were, they lived like British subjects. In this way and beyond, kingdom citizens should be distinct from their culture. It is this distinction that earns the contempt of society. In *Rumors of Another World*, Philip Yancey writes, "No one gets an exemption from hardship on planet Earth. How we receive it hinges on whether we believe in an alternate reality, that transcends the one we know so well."[2] As citizens of the kingdom, we should believe in that alternate reality and live our lives accordingly.

Expanded translation

You are blessed when you are being harassed because of your emphasis on internal righteousness and external justice. The kingdom of heaven is made up of people like you.

> μακάριοί ἐστε ὅταν ὀνειδίσωσιν ὑμᾶς
> καὶ διώξωσιν καὶ εἴπωσιν πᾶν πονηρὸν καθ' ὑμῶν
> ψευδόμενοι ἕνεκεν ἐμοῦ χαίρετε καὶ ἀγαλλιᾶσθε
> ὅτι ὁ μισθὸς ὑμῶν πολὺς ἐν τοῖς οὐρανοῖς
> οὕτως γὰρ ἐδίωξαν
> τοὺς προφήτας τοὺς πρὸ ὑμῶν

> Blessed are you when they reproach you
> and persecute and say all evil against you
> lying for the sake of me. Rejoice and be glad
> because your reward [is] great in heaven
> for thus they persecuted
> the prophets [the ones] before you.

Matthew 5:11-12 · The Results of Action, part 2

Lied About and Insulted

Although in the expanded translations thus far I have written, "you are blessed," this verse is the first one in which Jesus addresses his hearers directly. Verses 3-10 begin "Blessed are the ones...." Verse 11 begins "you [pl.] are blessed...." Jesus is getting personal.

Understanding the Greek in these verses fills in the background and adds depth to our knowledge. *Oneidizo*, the word translated "reproach," means finding fault in a way that demeans another, mocking, and heaping insults as a way of shaming. This is the same word used in Matthew 27:44 of the insults shouted at Jesus by the robbers crucified with him.

The word for "persecute" is the same word used in the last verse—*dediogmeno*. The word used for "evil" is *poneron*. This does not mean active wickedness as much as bad in a moral sense, worthless, base, and cowardly. It leans toward vicious. Both *oneidizo* and *poneron* indicate a kind of childish, spiteful malice.

The Message says in part, "What it means is that the truth is too close for comfort and they are uncomfortable." The behavior being described is what people indulge in when they are angry but don't have anything real of which to accuse the other. They spit out insults and say nasty, harmful words. It is the way we act when our pride is hurt or we know we are in the wrong but don't want to admit it, or when we feel convicted and are angry because of it.

I often hear this behavior on the bus from three middle school boys who ride at the same time I do every morning. Most of the time their conversation is simple one-upmanship—I'm better, stronger, faster, or whatever—but occasionally a serious accusation hits. Then the tone changes from "I'm superior," to "You're wrong and here's why, you so-and-so." Unfortunately, we sometimes don't leave that behavior behind in childhood.

We see it constantly in politicians who slap labels on the opposition for the sole purpose of making their opponents look bad. We hear it in racial slurs, gender slurs, and economic slurs. We hear it every time someone labels another "fanatic," or even "terrorist." We may experience insults, name-calling, and lies for a variety of reasons, but when they come because we are living with morals and values that cause others discomfort, it is then that we are called blessed.

In Good Company

Jesus says that when we are persecuted for the right reasons, we are being blessed by God. More than that, he says we should rejoice. This is definitely not a normal reaction to mistreatment, but the verb form used is the imperative—the tense used when giving an order. "Rejoice!" Jesus says. The word *chairo* here indicates a state of happiness or well-being, the way we feel when everything is going our way. It is followed by an even stronger verb, *agalliao*, which means being exceedingly joyful and glad. As *The Message* puts it, "Give a cheer." This is not some mild, half-hearted reaction. When we are harassed, insulted, and lied about for Jesus' sake, we should be thrilled like we often are on Christmas or when we receive the very birthday present we longed for. Talk about turning conventional wisdom on its head! This may be the hardest attitude of all.

The other reason we must rejoice is because it shows we are on the right track. "For in the same way they persecuted the prophets who were before you." The prophets—those who speak for God—have always been persecuted. We remember the stories of Elijah running from Jezebel, Jeremiah in the well, John the Baptist's beheading, and Jesus' crucifixion. There were other martyrs of the early church, such as Joan of Arc and Martin Luther, along with all the others who suffered during the Reformation including such secular prophets as Galileo. Mary Dyer was hanged in colonial Boston, Massachusetts, Dietrich Bonhoffer was killed in a German prison camp, and many others suffer today. Being a prophet—a truth teller—is never a popular occupation. I'm reminded of Richard Rohr's *Everything Belongs* in which Rohr reminds us that Jesus has three stated roles of prophet, priest, and king. The church has accepted the priestly role and celebrates the kingly role, "but I've never, in all the Christian world, found a church named Christ the Prophet," he writes. "Nor is there any feast day called Christ the Prophet."[3] Prophets are called to make people uncomfortable, make them question, help the sacred break into the secular, and show the purely secular world for the pale, shallow thing it is. No wonder prophets are unpopular! And when we act the part of true citizens of the kingdom, we face the same unpopularity.

Jesus gives a second reason we should be so excited by this ill treatment: we can expect a great *misthos* in heaven. This word is usually translated as "reward," but that's not quite right. Instead, it means "remuneration for work done" or "wages." It can mean "reward," but only in the sense that the reward is earned. This is not the same word used in Romans 6:23 about the wages of sin, however; that is another Greek word used for the compensation due to a soldier.

How do we take this phrase that is literally translated, "great [are] the wages of you"? Does it mean Christians will be amply repaid in good things when they get to heaven? Perhaps. Remember that Matthew wrote during a time of great persecution in the church, and the early believers needed to hear these words of hope even more than we do today. Like an ambassador to a poor and unstable country who suffers hardships but does his duty, we look forward to the time when we return to our wonderful homeland where things are so much better.

Expanded translation

> You are blessed whenever people mock, insult, revile, harass, and say nasty, untrue things about you because you are mine. Living as citizens of God's kingdom, you are an affront to their whole way of life. Rejoice—and I mean be absolutely thrilled—because heaven is more than worth it. And when you are persecuted you'll know you're on the right track, because that's exactly how people have always treated those who speak for God here on earth.

4

αβγδεζηθικλμνξοπϱσςτυφχψωαβγδεζηθικλμνξοπϱσςτυφχψωαβγδεζηθικλμνξοπϱσςτυφχψω

SALT AND LIGHT

ὑμεῖς ἐστε τὸ ἅλας τῆς γῆς
ἐὰν δὲ τὸ ἅλας μωρανθῇ
ἐν τίνι ἁλισθήσεται
εἰς οὐδὲν ἰσχύει ἔτι
εἰ μὴ βληθὲν ἔξω
καταπατεῖσθαι ὑπὸ τῶν ἀνθρώπων

You are the salt of the earth.
But if the salt has become tasteless
by what shall it be made salty?
For nothing is it competent longer
except being cast out
to be trodden on by people.

Matthew 5:13 · Salty Christians

Ho, ev'ry one that is thirsty in spirit,
Ho, ev'ry one that is weary and sad;
Come to the fountain, there's fullness in Jesus,
All that you're longing for, come and be glad.

"I will pour water on him that is thirsty,
I will pour floods upon the dry ground;
Open your heart for the gift I am bringing;
While you are seeking Me, I will be found."

(Lucy R. Meyer, "Ho, Every One That is Thirsty In Spirit")

"You are the salt of the earth," Jesus says. What does that mean? You may have heard the saying, "She's just the salt of the earth," referring to someone who is very kind and always ready to help. Is that what Jesus means here? Not entirely.

In ancient times, salt was mainly used as a preservative. Typically, preserving was done exclusively at the temple, which had a monopoly on salt.[1] A farmer would bring an animal and pay the temple to kill it and preserve it for him. This not only ensured that the butchering was done correctly by skilled men, but also provided wealth for the temple.

Salt was precious and was often used for trade and barter. Roman soldiers received part of their pay in salt, which is where the expression "worth his salt" originated. Salt was used as seasoning for food. It is necessary for life; our bodies contain roughly the same ratio of salt as seawater contains—about 3.5 percent.

While I pondered the meaning of Matthew 5:13, a voice whispered in my heart that salt makes people thirsty. It struck me: We are called to make people thirsty for God, the living water.

The best thing about this living water is that it is free to all. As Isaiah 55:1 says, "Come, all you who are thirsty, come to the waters; and you who have no money, come, buy and eat! Come, buy wine and milk without money and without cost."

Twice in the gospels Jesus refers to living water. The first is when he speaks with a Samaritan woman at a well (John 4:13-14). Jesus tells her, "Everyone who drinks this water will be thirsty again, but whoever drinks the water I give him will never thirst. Indeed, the water I give him will become in him a spring of water welling up to eternal life." The second reference is found in John 7:37. On the last and most important day of the Festival of Booths, Jesus stood in the temple courtyard and said loudly, "If anyone is thirsty, let him come to me and drink." Thus we must make people thirsty, and God will give them the water that will become in them "a spring of water welling up to eternal life."

How do we make people thirsty for God? It is by living the life described in the Beatitudes. As the sermon is presented in a logical progression from verse to verse, Jesus might have started verse 13 by saying, "To describe what I've just said as a metaphor, you are the salt of the earth."

When Jesus was acting as salt, he was intriguing. Going back to the Samaritan woman at the well, Jesus says provocatively, "If you knew the gift of God and who it is that asks you for a drink, you would have asked him and he would have given you living water." By talking to her as a person he piques her curiosity and is able to lead her into a deeper discussion of spiritual things. Or take Nicodemus, who comes to Jesus by night. Jesus radically and cryptically tells Nicodemus, "No one can see the kingdom of God unless he is born again." This, too, leads them into a deep spiritual discussion.

At the same time, we don't have to confront people to be acting as salt. Often living as citizens of the kingdom is enough. Think of potato chips, or pretzels, or popcorn. When we eat them, we naturally become thirsty. So it should be with us as we live out our kingdom values before others.

Since the "you" is plural in this verse—you (plural) are the salt of the earth—perhaps we must ask whether our churches make visitors hungry and thirsty to know more of this God we serve. Do we make strangers welcome? Is it clear that our Christianity makes a real difference in our lives? Or do we ignore newcomers or worse, turn them off with our gossip and complaining? Do they see us as different from any other club they might walk into? Do *we* think of our faith community as an outpost of the kingdom? Are we reaching out to each other? To visitors? To our communities? To the world?

All who follow Christ are the salt of the earth. Although each grain of salt is necessary, only when used in a group do they make a difference. Part of being a Christ-follower involves being part of a community.

Expanded translation

You are the salt of the earth, but if the salt has lost the very characteristic that made it valuable, how shall it be turned back into salt? It is no longer serving any useful purpose and will be thrown out to be trampled into the ground by passersby. In the same way, if you aren't making people thirst for the living water, you are not serving your proper purpose and are useless to bring people to me.

> ὑμεῖς ἐστε τὸ φῶς τοῦ κόσμου
> οὐ δύναται πόλις κρυβῆναι
> ἐπάνω ὄρους κειμένη

You are the light of the earth.
It is not possible a city to hide
upon a mountain being set.

Matthew 5:14 · God's City Blazes With Light

We are the light of the world, Jesus says next. The word for "light" refers to items that give light, such as lanterns, torches, or lamps, in the way we might say, "Bring the light over here," when we mean, "Move the lamp closer."

The salt of the last section was to make people thirsty for the living water. Here the metaphor is more profound. Jesus is the light of the world, and we are the light of the world. We are to *be* Jesus to this sin-darkened world.

If we think of this world as dark, what brings light? Acting in kindness and helpfulness, being honest and having integrity, showing cheerfulness in the face of our normal daily routine, and having joy in times of adversity. The apostle Paul gave us the best list in Galatians 5:22-23, also called the Fruits of the Spirit: "But the fruit of the Spirit is love, joy, peace, patience, kindness, goodness, faithfulness, gentleness and self-control." Such are the crops the Holy Spirit grows within us when we allow it.

In many ways, salt and light are the same—they are things God brings to fruition inside us. But they are different, too. Salt offers a chance, a hope, and a possibility. For the lost son, it was the memory of his father's generosity that made him thirsty to go home. The father's forgiveness, however, was the light of grace, welcoming him back into the family. Perhaps the verses are in this order because we start by making people thirsty and as they learn more and we grow in grace, we begin to glow with God's light for those who can see it.

Though generally salt is salt, there are many different types of lights. Night-lights keep us from stubbing our toes in the dark. Flashlights help us find our way outdoors. Incandescent bulbs let us work even when it's dark. Floodlights show everything in sharp detail. Lighthouses keep ships safe at sea, protecting them from the rocks of the shore. Neon lights flash before us and make announcements. Traffic lights regulate traffic. Infrared lights keep our hamburgers warm. Ultraviolet lights help our plants grow. Cathode rays let us see our televisions or computers. Christmas lights help celebrate Jesus' birth. Candles provide romantic atmosphere. With different personality types and different gifts, we each have our own unique way to show God's love to those around us. When we are all doing our part, Jesus says, we become like a city set on high ground, blazing with light—a city that can be seen for miles around.

But if we don't shine, there will be darkness. As there are many kinds of light, there are many different kinds of darkness. There is the darkness of a beautiful summer night, with its glorious array of stars and moon; the fearful darkness of a cave or a room without windows; the claustrophobia of fog at night; and the darkness of deliberately blocked light, such as closed eyes. Light can dispel any darkness except the last, bringing color and balance and joy. As I think of the great darkness covering the world today, I wonder how we can shine more brightly and how we can help chase that darkness away.

Another characteristic of light is that it doesn't glow without outside power. I can have dozens or even hundreds of lights in my living room, but until I get up and flip the switch or light a match, I'm as much in the dark as if there were none. Stars, including our own sun, have power in themselves, as God has power. But we lesser lights must be given power, and even the stars have only power as God has granted. We can only be lights for God when we have the Holy Spirit within us. There is, however, one difference between us and candles or lightbulbs—we can choose not to shine, as we will see in the next verse.

οὐδὲ καίουσιν λύχνον καὶ τιθέασιν αὐτὸν
ὑπὸ τὸν μόδιον ἀλλ' ἐπὶ τὴν λυχνίαν
καὶ λάμπει πᾶσιν τοῖς ἐν τῇ οἰκίᾳ

Nor do they light a lamp and place it
under the clay pot but on the lamp stand
and it lightens all the ones in the house

Matthew 5:15 · Christian Lamps

This little light of mine,
I'm gonna let it shine.
This little light of mine,
I'm gonna let it shine.
This little light of mine,
I'm gonna let it shine.
Let it shine,
Let it shine,
Let it shine.

Hide it under a bushel? No!
I'm gonna let it shine.
Hide it under a bushel? No!
I'm gonna let it shine.
Hide it under a bushel? No!
I'm gonna let it shine.
Let it shine,
Let it shine,
Let it shine.

(variation on an old spiritual)

Jesus now speaks to individuals. "Nor do they light a lamp," this verse begins. The lamp here is not a candle, but rather a small oil lamp. It is a lamp that can be picked up and carried and was often set in a lamp stand. These stands may hold several lamps; for example, the one in the temple held seven. Therefore, we might think of this as something like the city metaphor where multiple lights join together for brighter illumination in the sin-darkness of this world.

Instead of putting the lamp on a lamp stand, we can choose instead to hide it under a *modios*. This is translated "bushel" in the Authorized Version of the Bible. When I was a child, I used to picture a small basket over a candle, which never made sense to me. However, Jesus is likely referring to a clay pot, the kind used for storage. Putting a light under a clay pot isn't such a far-fetched idea; Gideon and his men did so to sneak up on the Midian army (Judges 7). Unlike the torches of Gideon's army, however, the good news we bear from God is not meant to be a secret. Rather, it is to be shouted from the rooftops, or, as this verse says, put on a lamp stand.

Clay pots were also used to preserve. They did it well—witness the Dead Sea Scrolls, still intact after centuries. However, we often take the precious light of God within us and try to hide it in order to preserve it from outside dangers. The problem with trying to preserve a light in this way is that not only does it no longer perform its purpose, but if you seal a lamp in a pot, the light will go out, accomplishing nothing. We must keep our wick trimmed and our oil well filled that the Holy Spirit may shine through us.

On whom are we to shine? All those in the room. A lamp doesn't pick and choose where to shine. It doesn't say, "You've been good today so I'll be sure to give you good light for reading." Nor can it decide, "You are naughty so I'll keep you in the dark." No! A lamp's job is to shine and not pass judgment. In just such a way, we are to live as Christ followers everywhere and with everyone.

οὕτως λαμψάτω τὸ φῶς ὑμῶν ἔμπροσθεν τῶν ἀνθρώπων ὅπως ἴδωσιν ὑμῶν τὰ καλὰ ἔργα καὶ δοξάσωσιν τὸν πατέρα ὑμῶν τὸν ἐν τοῖς οὐρανοῖς

Thus shine your light before the
people so that they may see your good works and
glorify your Father in heaven.

Matthew 5:16 · Making it Personal

Having compared us to salt and light, Jesus now moves on to make sure we understand. This verse is usually translated by some variation on the anemic, "Let your light shine." However, the verb Christ uses is imperative, the tense used for a command. This isn't a suggestion. "Shine your [pl.] light!" Jesus orders. We are to shine in the presence of other people, not to glorify ourselves but to help others understand why we behave as we do. The phrase "good works" might perhaps better be understood as the beautiful, useful service we do for others.

If our light is shining—if we are not shy about who we are and whom we serve—then what we say and do will be seen by others and cause them to think well of the God we serve. We need to remember that at all times we are God's ambassadors to this world, always in the public eye and always living our God-centered lives for the good of those around us. There should be no such thing as a "closet" Christian. At the same time, we can take heart that all the *you*s in this verse are plural. Christianity is meant to be a community affair. Many grains of salt make people thirsty. Many different kinds of light make the city glow. When we work together with Jesus as our guide, we can do great things.

There's an old illustration about a preacher who visits a farmer. The farmer asks why he should bother going to church. Without a word, the preacher picks up a pair of tongs and removes a piece of coal from the fire, setting it alone on the hearth. As they continue to talk, it dims and turns cold. This is not just a parable about joining with other believers on Sunday, but about us becoming stronger, brighter, and more effective when we work together. Alone, we fade and grow dim and cold. No one can be truly effective by himself. Tom Sine devotes much space to a discussion of Christian community in the third section of *Mustard Seed Versus McWorld*: "I believe the church at its best is called to be a new community centered in the worship of the living God…sharing life and resources as would a large extended family."[2] He advocates Christians spending more time together, not to create a Christian ghetto, but to encourage and strengthen one another as they live out Sermon-on-the-Mount values. Let us covenant with our fellow Christ followers and work together to make the world thirsty for God and to light the way to our Savior.

Expanded translation

> You are carriers of my light to the world. A city placed on a hill cannot be kept secret. Nor do I, God, put the light of my Spirit within you secretly, but I put you where all can see the bright light in you, and, through you, catch a glimpse of me. Shine that light before others, making God attractive to all you meet by your grace-full lifestyle.

5

EVERYTHING OLD IS NEW AGAIN

μὴ νομίσητε ὅτι ἦλθον καταλῦσαι τὸν νόμον
ἢ τοὺς προφήτας
οὐκ ἦλθον καταλῦσαι ἀλλὰ πληρῶσαι

Believe not that I came to annul the law
or the prophets
I came not to annul but to fulfill.

Matthew 5:17 · Jesus as the Fulfillment of Prophecy

The sermon seems to take an abrupt turn here as Jesus suddenly begins talking about the law and the prophets—the Old Testament. In actuality, it is not so much a right angle as a curve. The next few verses serve as another transition in the sermon. Jesus moves from reminding us about our call to shine our lights and to make people thirst for the living water to a discussion of several specific laws and their interpretation. Although this passage can be difficult to understand, it is also exciting as we get to hear Jesus' point of view on the Old Testament.

I love to listen to authors talk about their lives and their work. I've heard Madeleine L'Engle speak about juggling her home life and caring for small children, with her professional life as she wrote

A Wrinkle in Time. Isaac Asimov once came to my area to talk about his rose-colored vision of the future. Hearing Stephen Hawking live was one of the high points of my life, especially waiting as he composed his answers during the question time after his speech. At a meeting of new science fiction authors, Ursula K. Le Guin discussed how and why her fiction had changed from masculine themes to a more feminine view of the universe. The more we know about a writer the more we understand his or her work, especially when the author explains what he or she has written and why. In the same way, the next few verses give us a privileged glimpse into the Old Testament as its author discusses its meaning.

"Don't make the mistake of believing I've come to annul all the previous communication between God and human beings," Jesus begins. He knows how easy it is for us to run after the new and reject the old. We see it when we have to add the newest fashion to a closet already bulging with clothing that was perfectly good last month. We see it when we have to buy the newest cell phone because of cool new features. One year we love Cabbage Patch dolls; another it's Pokémons. We buy this detergent because it's new and improved, or switch to that brand of toothpaste to get the whitest smile.

People were no different two thousand years ago. They wanted to follow this miracle worker with his new religion. But Jesus was not the newest fad. He was not the harbinger of a new religion, nor was he bringing something new and improved.

Instead, Jesus is what God had been planning all along. The entire Old Testament finds its fulfillment in Christ. God had been giving human beings the message of love repeatedly through Moses and the prophets, and now God is here to give it in person.

The verb *pléroó* has the basic meaning "to fill." However, one of the extended meanings is especially appropriate here: "to bring to completion an activity in which one has been involved from the beginning."[1] Jesus did not come to make the Old Testament invalid; he came to finish what he started and explain what he had been doing all along.

Expanded translation

Do not believe as others do that I was sent here by heaven for the purpose of annulling all the words of God you have received through the years. I am the one who gave you those messages. Now I am the completion of them. I am what those messages have always been about.

ἀμὴν γὰρ λέγω ὑμῖν
ἕως ἂν παρέλθῃ ὁ οὐρανὸς καὶ ἡ γῆ
ἰῶτα ἓν ἢ μία κεραία οὐ μὴ
παρέλθῃ ἀπὸ τοῦ νόμου ἕως ἂν
πάντα γένηται

For truly I say to you
until pass away the heavens and the earth
one iota or one point by no means
shall pass away from the law until
all things come to pass.

Matthew 5:18 · God's Words Last

This is a difficult verse to interpret. Could it mean that for those who live by the Old Testament, such as the Jews, the law remains permanently in force, but for Christians, who live by the New Testament, the law no longer applies? Or could it mean instead that the moral law will never pass away but the ceremonial law has been surpassed? A champion of the first interpretation is Robert Guelich in his book *The Sermon on the Mount*.[2] There are equally strong defenders of the second interpretation.

In Matthew 5:18, Jesus prepares to give several examples of what the laws really mean: the point was never the outward symbols, but the inward attitude; never the rituals, but the love for our great and merciful God. This is confirmed in Mark 12:32-33 when the scribe says to Jesus, "Teacher, that was well said! You've told the truth that there is only one God and no other besides him! To love him with all your heart, with all your understanding, with all your strength, and to love your neighbor as yourself is more important than all the burnt offerings and sacrifices." Though the specifics of the law may change over time (indeed, we see that in the Bible itself), the truth behind it—God's love for us and our response to that love—will never change.

Through all the elaborate rituals, through the trappings added by men, through the misunderstandings, the truth is the same now as it was in the beginning. Whatever its formula, the purpose of the law is to lead us to God. Though people have sometimes kept only the letter of the law—for example, the Pharisees—its spirit remained intact. Though people often lift verses out of context and use them to justify actions directly opposite the spirit, the intent still survives. Through the years people have added to, twisted, mistranslated, and misunderstood God's word to us, but that doesn't invalidate it. Our job is to try our best to understand and then to live our lives according to that light.

Expanded translation

Believe this truth: I declare to you that until this universe comes to an end and disappears, not even one dot or a single stroke shall disappear from God's written communication to you. However, listen closely to what I am going to be telling you shortly. I will explain to you the way the law was intended to be understood from the beginning.

ὃς ἐὰν οὖν λύσῃ μίαν
τῶν ἐντολῶν τούτων τῶν ἐλαχίστων καὶ
διδάξῃ οὕτως τοὺς ἀνθρώπους ἐλάχιστος
κληθήσεται
ἐν τῇ βασιλείᾳ τῶν οὐρανῶν
ὃς δ' ἂν ποιήσῃ καὶ διδάξῃ οὗτος μέγας
κληθήσεται ἐν τῇ βασιλείᾳ τῶν οὐρανῶν

Whoever therefore annuls one
of these commandments the least and
teaches thus people, least
shall be called
in the kingdom of the heavens
but whoever keeps and teaches this one great
shall be called in the kingdom of the heavens.

Matthew 5:19 · A Warning to Teachers

Who is Jesus talking about here? It seems likely that, since Jesus specifically names the Pharisees and teachers of the law in the next verse, he is speaking to them.

In Greek, the verb *lusé* means much more than "break." It indicates deliberate action and means "to destroy or abolish." This warning is not directed toward someone who accidentally messes up, but rather to the person who twists God's words deliberately.

In Jesus' warning, he speaks specifically to teachers: those in power who not only manipulate God's words to their benefit, but encourage others to think in the same way. We see this in:

- The Pharisees who taught that outward show was everything.
- The priests who twisted God's meanings so badly they couldn't recognize the Messiah when he came.
- Saul and others who persecuted God's followers in God's name.

- Those involved in the Inquisition who "converted" people at the point of a sword.
- People who use the Bible to justify slavery.
- Husbands who use the Bible to justify mistreatment of their wives.
- Fathers who use the Bible to justify mistreatment of their children.
- Anyone who *uses* people rather than *loves* them, for the most important commandment is to love others.

Jesus teaches that it is bad enough to deliberately distort the Scripture for your own ends, but teaching others to do the same is worse. If you do this you will be called least in the kingdom. The Greek verb *kaleo* indicates more than our English word *call*. It means "to name," that is, to call by one's true name and to name what someone really is. The best way to express this in English is that he "shall be called least in the kingdom of heaven—because he *is* least." Even to such people, however, God shows mercy. They aren't locked or cast out of the kingdom, but simply the least of its citizens.

The opposite of this teaching is also true. Whoever keeps the commandments—living a life of actively practicing love to others—shall be called great in the kingdom of heaven, especially if he or she teaches others to live likewise in this higher way. Not the greatest, for that is Jesus, but great—a true honor.

My best friend, Bonnie, was a teacher. She not only showed her preschoolers a lot of love but helped them learn how to get along with each other and grow socially, morally, and mentally. Bonnie gave herself to children in order to provide them with a good start in life. I'm sure that right now she is being called great in heaven, and if there are any children with her there she is in the middle of them, enjoying herself immensely.

If we aim to be more than least in the kingdom, we need to look carefully at how we treat God's words to us. We need to face our actions honestly and see if they meet the test of loving God and loving our neighbor. Those in authority must be especially careful, for the Bible teaches that with authority comes responsibility. There is no better role model than Jesus, the greatest in the kingdom.

Expanded translation

> Consequently, anyone who deliberately breaks or twists one of the least of God's commands, especially if he teaches people to do the same, shall be called least in God's kingdom—because he is least. But whoever keeps God's commands and teaches others to do the same shall be called great in the kingdom of heaven.

λέγω γὰρ ὑμῖν ὅτι ἐὰν μὴ περισσεύσῃ
ὑμῶν ἡ δικαιοσύνη πλεῖον τῶν
γραμματέων καὶ Φαρισαίων οὐ μὴ
εἰσέλθητε εἰς τὴν βασιλείαν τῶν οὐρανῶν

For I tell you that except shall greatly surpass
your righteousness greater than
the scribes and Pharisees by no means
shall you enter into the kingdom of heaven.

Matthew 5:20 · Inward and Outward Righteousness

The Bible contains many statements that seem to go against logic. The person who tries to save his or her life will lose it. Love your enemies. Don't worry about material possessions. This verse contains another. The teachers of the law and the Pharisees were the super-spiritual men of their day. In today's world, they are those who collect stories of all the sinners they have helped. They are those everybody looks up to because they continually win converts; go deeper into one discipline or another; and pray longer than anyone else, with just the right tone of voice and all the right religious vocabulary. The church looks up to them and values their opinions. They are spiritual legends. Yet Jesus says our righteousness must be greater than this.

Here, Jesus describes not the true saints of the church, but those more concerned about how others will perceive them than whether or not they obey God.

The good news is that God isn't looking for that type of feigned super Christian. Instead, the Beatitudes describe the sort of person God looks for: humble, not flashy; peacemakers, not scene-stealers; and merciful, not self-righteous and judgmental. God looks for two kinds of righteousness: an attitude that begins with *inward* righteousness and getting our heart right with God, and moves second to *outward* acts of righteousness such as loving others, working for justice for the powerless, and being peacemakers.

Why is this more than the righteousness of the super spiritual? The Pharisees performed all the correct rituals but for all the wrong reasons. Jesus will soon begin a long discussion about how the laws have been twisted and how only our inner attitudes truly matter. It is the intent of the heart that is significant in the end, providing that that intent leads to action. Faith without works is dead, but works without faith and love are meaningless in the heavenly ledger. They are, as Paul says later in 1 Corinthians 13, only noise like a gong or a cymbal, or, as Macbeth says, "full of sound and fury, and signifying nothing."[3]

Chances of entering the kingdom of heaven in this case are nil—Matthew uses the emphatic negative here. Those who have twisted the words of God are least in the kingdom, but those with only outward righteousness don't get in at all. Later in chapter 6, Jesus calls these people playactors, and that's the key. Those who play the part of a super-spiritual person with no love beneath can't get into the kingdom because they don't understand its purpose.

Expanded translation

> Let me be more specific. I'm telling you that unless your righteousness—both your private worship of God and your reaching out to others in God's name—is much more sincere than the outward show of righteousness of the law experts and their followers, the Pharisees, you don't understand what it means to be a citizen of the kingdom of heaven. Now listen carefully, because I'm going to give you some examples of what I mean.

6

αβγδεζηθικλμνξοπςστυφχψωαβγδεζηθικλμνξοπςστυφχψωαβγδεζηθικλμνξοπςστυφχψω

The First Law

MURDER & ANGER

(Sins of the Mind)

The Six Antitheses

From this point on in Matthew 5 (verse 21 and following), Jesus offers examples to illustrate what he said previously about the law and righteousness. He begins by referring back to a specific command and then explaining the true meaning of that command, thereby showing that the law was never meant to be a set of external rules but instead sets forth principles for the actions that arise from a heart attuned to God.

All of these sections begin the same way: "You have been taught that it was said by [or *told to*] your ancestors [the people of olden times]...," though sometimes "your ancestors" is understood rather than explicitly stated. This is followed a verse later by "But (or *and*) I am proclaiming to you...."

There are several contrasts in these sets of statements besides the clearly stated one:

- The verses referring to the law contain a passive verb: it *was said*. When Jesus speaks, he uses the active voice: I *am proclaiming* to you.
- The verb in both cases is *lego*, or "to say." When referring to the law, it is in past tense. Jesus uses the present tense for his explanations.
- The citing of the law is an appeal to tradition. Jesus speaks with his own authority.

The verbs here are a little slippery, with a wide range of meanings. *Akouó*, "to hear," can also mean "to understand," "to learn," or "to be taught." Jesus isn't so much saying "That was then, this is now," as "This is what you were taught, and here's what it really means." *Lego* most simply means, "to say," but has a range of stronger translations. It can mean, "to declare," "to tell," "to proclaim," "to report," or "to explain." To stay consistent with Jesus' role as Messiah, I have chosen to translate *lego* as "to proclaim."

In brief, the last part of Matthew 5:

The Law says	**I, Jesus, proclaim**
Don't murder.	Don't let your anger get the better of you.
Don't commit adultery.	Don't even consider women in this light.
If you divorce your wife, give her a certificate of divorce.	Don't divorce your wife for any reason but unfaithfulness.
Don't break your oath.	Don't swear at all.
Don't go overboard with vengeance.	Meet wrongdoing with creative nonviolence.
Love your friends.	Love everybody.

ἠκούσατε ὅτι ἐρρέθη
τοῖς ἀρχαίοις οὐ φονεύσεις ὃς δ' ἂν
φονεύσῃ ἔνοχος ἔσται τῇ κρίσει ἐγὼ δὲ
λέγω ὑμῖν ὅτι
πᾶς ὁ ὀργιζόμενος τῷ ἀδελφῷ αὐτοῦ ἔνοχος ἔσται
τῇ κρίσει ὃς δ' ἂν εἴπῃ
τῷ ἀδελφῷ αὐτοῦ ῥακά ἔνοχος ἔσται τῷ συνεδρίῳ
ὃς δ' ἂν εἴπῃ μωρέ
ἔνοχος ἔσται εἰς τὴν γέενναν τοῦ πυρός

You have been taught that it was said
by those of old, "You shall not murder and whoever
commits a murder will be liable to the court." But
I am proclaiming to you that
anyone being furious with his brother will be liable
to the court. And whoever says
to his brother "Idiot!" will be liable to the council.
And whoever says "Moron!"
shall be liable in the Gehenna of fire.

Matthew 5:21-22 · Don't Let Your Anger Get the Better of You

The old law in the Ten Commandments is straightforward for most of us. "Do not murder." The deliberate act of hunting down another human being to take his or her life is abhorrent to the vast majority of people. But Jesus looks around and says, "Stop congratulating yourselves. The law was never meant to be understood so narrowly." To break this law you don't have to kill someone but only be angry enough to do so.

"Whoever is angry with his brother is liable to the same judgment as a murderer," Jesus says. What does this mean? Any time I lose my temper, do I lose my salvation? If so, Paul could not have written in Ephesians 4:26, "In your anger do not sin," which he quotes from Psalm 4:4. The word for "anger" here, *orgizomenos*, means "strong displeasure with a focus on retribution" and is used to describe God's wrath at the final judgment. It is the anger that makes a person wish retribution would fall on the one who has wronged him or her. We might not allow ourselves to get angry enough to kill somebody, but we may get angry enough to hope *somebody* makes him or her pay.

We turn on the news and see this kind of anger rampant through the world. We see it between the Israelis and the Palestinians. We see it between the Islamic militants and those from the West. We see it in courtrooms directed at those who have dishonored, injured, or killed a loved one. We feel its stirrings when someone we trusted betrays us. No human being is immune.

Yet Jesus isn't finished. He mentions two other ways we seriously wrong others—by calling someone an idiot or a moron. The first word, *Raca*, is an Aramaic insult whose literal meaning is "empty one." I believe Jesus is expounding psychological rules here that we didn't come to understand until much later. When we insult someone, we damage his or her self-esteem in ways more painful and lasting than if we had hit that person physically. The second word, *moros*, means much the same: "dull, sluggish, stupid." Our word *moron* comes from this. Jesus may be saying the same thing two different ways, but where *Raca* attacks a person emotionally, *moros* is a general term of abuse. We might say the first is spoken to deliberately wound someone and the second the word of somebody mad at the world and habitually angry with no respect for others.

Respect is what this whole section of the sermon is about. As citizens of the kingdom, we are to respect our brother and sisters, women, the marriage vow, ourselves and others, our enemies, and those in need. We must act as children of God, here and now, in this world.

This is difficult for all of us. I have trouble seeing those on the bus as brothers and sisters: those who sit and curse the system, those who use drugs, those who abuse mentally and physically, those between jail times, and those who are drunk. There are also those who want to kill our nation's enemies; those who want the authority to rape the environment; those who refuse to see the plight of the poor as anything but their own fault; and those who complain about coworkers instead of helping them. We see evidence of self-centered lifestyles everywhere, all the time.

The verse's final phrase, "Gehenna of fire," does not mean "hell" as we often picture it. Gehenna was a place to throw garbage outside Jerusalem. Periodically the garbage was burned off to control the amount of refuse, and Gehenna came to be symbolic of the judgment of God. The symbolism in this verse suggests the stages of court appearances, going from lower to higher—anyone getting furious with his brother will be liable to the court, whoever calls his brother "Idiot!" will be liable to the council, and whoever says "Moron!" will be liable in Gehenna. Today we may be responsible to the circuit court, to the Supreme Court, and finally to the judgment of God.

Expanded translation

> You have been taught that it was said by your ancestors, "You shall not commit murder," and if anyone does commit a murder he shall be answerable to the law court and to human justice. I now proclaim to you that anyone who is furious with a fellow human being is answerable to the lower courts, and whoever deliberately destroys the self-esteem of another is answerable to the Supreme Court, and anyone who calls others uncomplimentary names shall be answerable for it at the final judgment.

ἐὰν οὖν προσφέρῃς τὸ δῶρόν σου
ἐπὶ τὸ θυσιαστήριον κἀκεῖ μνησθῇς ὅτι
ὁ ἀδελφός σου ἔχει τι κατὰ σοῦ
ἄφες ἐκεῖ τὸ δῶρόν σου ἔμπροσθεν τοῦ θυσιαστηρίου
καὶ ὕπαγε πρῶτον διαλλάγηθι τῷ ἀδελφῷ σου
καὶ τότε ἐλθὼν πρόσφερε τὸ δῶρόν σου

Therefore if you bring your gift
to the altar and there remember that
your brother has something against you
leave there your gift before the altar
and go first be reconciled to your friend
and then come offer your gift.

Matthew 5:23-24 · Take the Initiative to Make Things Right with Your Friends

Forgiving someone who hurts us isn't always easy, but we try because it is something we know we should do. Yet this verse isn't about someone who has wronged us. This is somebody who thinks we have wronged him or her: "your friend has something against you...."

How easy it is to be self-righteous. "If she thinks I'm crawling to her, she can forget it!" "She started it! If she wants my forgiveness, she's going to have to ask me for it." "I can't help what he thinks. I don't know where he ever got that idea about me anyway." "I'm not going to apologize—I didn't do anything wrong." Often, when someone thinks we have wronged him or her, it's our attitude that needs fixing.

Do we need to take the blame for everything? No. At the same time, this isn't about who to blame. It's not about who acted rightly or wrongly. It's about relationships and peacemaking. It's about reconciliation and bringing things back into balance by restoring relationships. It can mean apologizing even when we believe we are in the right, for we should at least be sorry for our role in the breakdown of the relationship. It can mean listening intently to understand the hurt, and doing what we can to put things right. But we can't force reconciliation. When the lost son returned home, he was reconciled to his father, but not to his brother.

Paul says in Romans 12:18 "If it is possible, as far as it depends on you, live at peace with everyone." God is our example. We sin against God again and again, yet our heavenly Parent is always there, making the first move, offering forgiveness and reconciliation. God is the shepherd who searches for the lost sheep and restores it to the flock and the woman who sweeps her entire house until she finds her lost coin. God actively searches for those of us who deliberately walk away—like the prodigal son—and rejoices when we return.

Practicing peacemaking also means trying to understand other people's feelings. It means swallowing my pride, or, as the Beatitudes put it, being humble and taking the first step. It means listening with my heart and doing what I can to put things right. And it means doing that now. When you are off to church, Jesus says, and suddenly remember that a friend has something against you, go and take care of that first, and then you can worship with a clear heart.

Peacemaking isn't just about healing relationships between people. Making things right with others helps us make things right with God so that we may worship God properly and hear God clearly.

Expanded translation

> If you are heading off to church to worship and on the way remember that a friend holds something against you, turn around and go make things right with that person first. Then you can come back and worship with a clear heart.

ἴσθι εὐνοῶν τῷ ἀντιδίκῳ σου ταχὺ
ἕως ὅτου εἶ μετ' αὐτοῦ ἐν τῇ ὁδῷ
μήποτέ σε παραδῷ ὁ ἀντίδικος τῷ κριτῇ
καὶ ὁ κριτὴς τῷ ὑπηρέτῃ καὶ εἰς φυλακὴν
βληθήσῃ ἀμὴν λέγω σοι
οὐ μὴ ἐξέλθῃς ἐκεῖθεν ἕως
ἂν ἀποδῷς τὸν ἔσχατον κοδράντην

Make friends with your adversary quickly
while you are with him in the way,
lest deliver you the adversary to the judge
and the judge to the bailiff and into prison
you be thrown. Truly I say to you
you shall by no means come out from there until
you have repaid every last cent [of your fine].

Matthew 5:25-26 · Take the Initiative to Make Things Right with Your Enemies

"Make friends with your enemy quickly," Jesus begins. Today we might say, "Look for common ground between you and the person who is constantly irritating you." We've all known people who rub us the wrong way or whom we rub the wrong way. Living or working with someone who is hypercritical is a special sort of trial. For some, it's a parent who is never pleased. For some it is a teacher who looks at all we do with an unfriendly eye. It could be an acquaintance, a relative, a spouse, a coworker, or a boss. Sometimes these critics can be ignored or taken with a grain of understanding; some we must find ways to tolerate.

This verse does not refer to situations such as child abuse—where the child has no power in relation to his or her abuser—nor situations where the abuser is mentally unbalanced. In such cases, victims need outside help. These verses refer to situations such as when a coworker constantly gossips about you and puts you down to others. Far more than a mere annoyance, she can make your work life a symbolic hell and make you doubt your own worth. So can a nagging spouse, a dictatorial boss, or an unfair parent. Jesus talks about your adversary dragging you into court, but that isn't necessarily a literal court of law. With your accuser setting himself as prosecuting attorney before a jury of coworkers, other students, or the rest of the family, a person can find herself condemned and sentenced before she knows what's happening.

What is our common response in these situations? We gather a group of friends and grumble about how wrong our opponent is, likely pointing out his or her faults. It makes us feel smugly self-righteous and sympathetically victimized. Is this human? Very. Is it helpful to resolving the situation? No.

"Go to your accuser," Jesus says. "Make friends if you can. Nip the problem in the bud. Be a peacemaker."

There are things we can't do in a situation like this. We can't force people to change their minds about us. We can't make them stop repeating slanders. We can't change their attitudes or the climate of our surroundings. If people could slander Jesus the sinless, there's plenty they can find to say about me, a far-from-sinless human being.

But we can change ourselves. We can look at others as God sees them, as beloved sons or daughters. We can try to understand what pain is driving them to strike out at us. We can take the initiative to put things right. Sometimes that means apologizing because a real (or perceived) wrong on our part could have begun the whole thing. Sometimes it means asking what we have done or asking them to help us understand what is wrong. It always means praying for others, and treating them like human beings. Does this always fix the problem or change our "enemies" into friends? No; some people don't want to change. But we can keep trying, for we are responsible for our own attitude and actions.

Notice the differences between problems with friends and troubles with someone who is not a friend. In the first case, we drop everything to try to heal the relationship. Here, Jesus teaches us about the second case: "Settle matters quickly with your adversary....Do it while you are still with him on the way." In other words, we watch for the chance to speak to our enemy. We want to do it "quickly," but not with so much urgency that it's even more important than our usual time with God, as the previous verse says. (If you are on your way to worship and remember that a friend has something against you....)

What is the *same* is that we take the initiative, not so much to heal the relationship—that comes later—but to keep things from getting out of hand. Because when situations *do* get out of hand, it doesn't matter anymore who was right and who was wrong. We can find ourselves on the receiving end of an unjust punishment, whether that's jail time or ostracism, a messy divorce, the loss of child custody, or any one of hundreds of unwelcome consequences that can affect us the rest of our life. As Jesus says, "I tell you the truth, you will not get out until you have paid the last penny."

Aren't humility and peacemaking worth the effort to escape that penalty?

Expanded translation

> When you meet someone who is ill disposed toward you, grab the initiative and take the chance to make things right. If you don't, this person will continue making things worse and you could find yourself being hauled into court (literally or figuratively), condemned and sentenced before you know it. Suddenly you're locked up or locked out. I'm telling you straight, you will never escape until you have paid the fine determined by the court to the very last cent.

7

αβγδεζηθικλμνξοπρςστυφχψωαβγδεζηθικλμνξοπρςστυφχψωαβγδεζηθικλμνξοπρςστυφχψω

The Second and Third Laws

THE MARRIAGE VOW

(Sins of the Senses)

ἠκούσατε ὅτι ἐρρέθη
οὐ μοιχεύσεις
ἐγὼ δὲ λέγω ὑμῖν ὅτι πᾶς ὁ βλέπων
γυναῖκα πρὸς τὸ ἐπιθυμῆσαι αὐτὴν
ἤδη ἐμοίχευσεν
αὐτὴν ἐν τῇ καρδίᾳ αὐτοῦ

You have heard that it was said,
"Do not commit adultery."
But I am proclaiming to you that anyone looking
at a woman with a view to desire her
has already committed adultery
with her in his heart.

Matthew 5:27-28 · Don't Get Carried Away by Your Desire

The first law addressed our pride and the consequences we face when we are unwilling to be the first to make things right. This law warns us about letting our senses get us into trouble—what 1 John 2:16 calls "the lust of the eyes." Of the two groupings of sin, most of us tend to be tempted by one kind over the other. Sins of the mind include pride, greed, and judgmentalism; sins of the body include lust, gluttony, and drunkenness. The Jews had the Pharisees, tending toward the sins of the mind, and the Sadducees, tending toward the sins of the body. The Greeks had the Stoics and the Epicureans. People have always tended toward one sort of temptation over another.

Again Jesus begins with a law from the Ten Commandments: Do not commit adultery (Exodus 20:14). This is fairly straightforward and tied to a specific action: Don't break the marriage vow—your own or somebody else's. In Jesus' time single people were uncommon; a woman married at an early age and stayed married until her husband's death, so this command is meant for all adults and speaks to any sexual relations outside marriage.

There are many things to enjoy in this world of ours. Sunsets, walks on the beach, mountains, flowers, sunshine, rainbows, and animals: All are reminders of the richness of earth. Music, art, dance, and the joy of words well crafted are another kind of pleasure. Well-prepared food, beautifully handcrafted items—I could go on and on. People can also be beautiful to one another. Is Jesus saying if we notice the beauty in one another we have sinned? No.

The word for "look" in this verse is *blepo*. It means "to pay especially close attention, consider." The person doing the staring is taking a good, long look at another human being for the express purpose of thinking about him or her sexually. *The Message* captures the flavor of the words with its translation: "leering looks." Noticing is fine because it is natural that we should find one another attractive. When our imaginations get involved, however, we invite trouble. James 1:14-15 describes this perfectly: "But each one is tempted when, by his own evil desire, he is dragged away and enticed. Then, after desire has conceived, it gives birth to sin; and sin, when it is full-grown, gives birth to death." When we look long and hard and entertain ideas we should not, we get into trouble. Jesus' word is clear—don't entertain those thoughts. Shut the door and lock them out.

Why is lust called sin? First, specifically for adultery, we dishonor our spouse and break the vow given to him or her. Second, one of the major messages of the Sermon on the Mount is that we are to consider one another brothers and sisters, beloved children of our heavenly Parent. When someone becomes the object of lust, his or her humanity is eclipsed. Lust and respect cannot coexist. This is especially evident in the ugliest form of this sin—rape—where sex is used as a form of power to strike fear and shame into the victim. Lust is always about one person and his or her own desires.

Jesus' words about adultery are not new. Proverbs chapter 5 deals exclusively with this theme and suggests yet another reason to stay away from a person who excites lust. She—or he—may lead a person into an unsuitable relationship with a non-believer. Instead, as Proverbs 5:15 so coyly puts it, "Drink water from your own cistern."

Sexual lust is just one form of craving. Some people lust for power or control, addictive substances such as alcohol or narcotics, large amounts of certain foods, wealth, fame, danger or any number of things that can get hold of us and seem so important. Interestingly, the Greek word for "lust" comes from a word that means "to rush" as a stream rushes down a mountainside. When we surrender control to our emotions in places and at times we should not, we also surrender the better part of ourselves.

"Don't let your imagination get out of hand," Jesus says. "Don't stay in a position where this is likely to happen and don't let your desire get away from you, like a headlong rush down a mountain. You never know when you might run right off a cliff."

Indeed, Jesus takes lust very seriously.

Expanded translation

> You have heard that it was said: "Do not commit adultery." But I tell you that anyone who spends time gazing at another with sex in mind has already committed adultery in his or her heart and mind. Don't let your imagination and desires lead you into sin.

εἰ δὲ ὁ ὀφθαλμός σου ὁκ δεξιὸς σκανδαλίζει σε ἔξελε
αὐτὸν καὶ βάλε ἀπὸ σοῦ συμφέρει γάρ σοι
ἵνα ἀπόληται ἓν τῶν μελῶν σου καὶ μὴ
ὅλον τὸ σῶμά σου βληθῇ εἰς γέενναν
καὶ εἰ ἡ δεξιά σου χεὶρ σκανδαλίζει σε
ἔκκοψον αὐτὴν καὶ βάλε ἀπὸ σοῦ συμφέρει γάρ
σοι ἵνα ἀπόληται ἓν τῶν μελῶν σου
καὶ μὴ ὅλον τὸ σῶμά σου εἰς γέενναν ἀπέλθῃ

And if your right eye causes you to stumble, pluck
it out and throw it from you. For it is better for you
that should perish one of your members and not
all your body be thrown onto Gehenna.
And if your right hand causes you to stumble,
sever it and throw it from you. For it is better
for you that should perish one of your members
and not all your body onto Gehenna depart.

Matthew 5:29-30 · Drastic Problems Require Drastic Remedies

It is clear Jesus takes sin seriously. In order to break its power over us, Jesus allowed himself to be killed by the worst method of death inflicted by the judicial system of his time. Although he is in the early part of his ministry as he preaches this sermon and no one, not even his disciples, dreams about what could be coming, Jesus already knows what human sin is going to do to him.

Matthew 5:29-30 points back to the previous verses, specifically speaking of temptation to sexual sin. At the same time, there are many kinds of temptations and many forms of sin. In the Greek, the verses' verbs are in the present tense, indicating repeated action. Jesus is talking about a problem that continues and can only be solved by drastic measures. "If your right eye repeatedly causes your downfall...." "If your right hand continuously causes you to stumble...." The eye stands for the mind, specifically long, lustful looks, and the hand for wrongful action. Both are equally condemned. The verse goes on: "pluck out [your eye]" or "sever [your hand]." Jesus uses exaggeration to prove a point.

A few years ago there was a popular saying, "The devil made me do it." It made us laugh, especially Flip Wilson's delivery, but many people buy into that belief. Some also believe the opposite: "If God really wanted me to be good, God wouldn't put this temptation in my way," or, "God is testing me." Many of us would agree with Oscar Wilde: "I can resist anything except temptation." For the most part, however, we fall because we ourselves open the door to sin. In James 1:13-15 we read, "When tempted, no one should say, 'God is tempting me.' For God cannot be tempted by evil, nor does he tempt anyone; but each one is tempted when, by his own evil desire, he is dragged away and enticed. Then, after desire has conceived, it gives birth to sin; and sin, when it is full-grown, gives birth to death."

Temptation is serious; sin is serious. We need to remove ourselves from the places and activities that encourage us to sin. I have a friend to whom God gave the command, "Get rid of your television; your life depends on it." Adam and Eve's sin got them cast out of Paradise. When Moses struck the rock, against God's order, he lost his chance to enter the Promised Land. Whatever tempts us—or paradoxically, whatever gives us security—needs to be surrendered, plucked out, or cut off. To the wealthy young man who came to Jesus asking what he needed to do to have eternal life, the command was, "If you want to be perfect, go, sell your possessions and give to the poor" (Matthew 19:21). Though the young man lived a good life, his security was in his possessions. He could not give them up to follow Jesus. On the other hand, when God asked Abraham to give up his only son, he showed himself willing to obey.

Often I find security in clinging to the little money I have. God has been saying to me, "Don't worry, I'll take care of you—haven't I proved that over and over? Learn to be generous with what you have." It's a lesson I am trying hard to learn, but it's not easy. We are all tempted in different ways—security, power, the need for love. What we must learn is that God is our security; God has all the power in the universe; and God loves us better than any human being ever could.

Sometimes things are relatively easy to give up and sometimes that process is as painful as maiming oneself. Abraham was rewarded for his faithfulness, heartwrenching though it was, but for the wealthy young man the command was too difficult, and he walked away sadly.

Jesus goes on to say that it's better to lose something precious to us than to end up thrown outside the city with the rest of the nasty garbage. The word translated "better" is interesting. It means, "confer a benefit, be profitable or useful." We could say it is better for our eternal profit margin to give up something precious to us here on earth than to be cast onto Gehenna and therefore be cut off from God and God's people, to be cast out of the kingdom, and to lose our chance of heaven.

These are hard words for us to hear today.

Expanded translation

> But if your right eye is constantly causing you to mess up morally, tear it out and throw it away from you. For it's a whole lot better in the long run that you lose one part of your body rather than that your entire body should be tossed onto the waste dump, where God doesn't go. And if your right hand is constantly causing you to mess up morally, chop it off and throw it away from you. For it's a whole lot better in the long run that you lose one part of your body rather than that your entire body should end up on the waste dump, where God doesn't go.

ἐρρέθη δέ ὃς ἂν ἀπολύσῃ τὴν γυναῖκα αὐτοῦ
δότω αὐτῇ ἀποστάσιον
ἐγὼ δὲ λέγω ὑμῖν ὅτι πᾶς ὁ ἀπολύων
τὴν γυναῖκα αὐτοῦ παρεκτὸς λόγου
πορνείας ποιεῖ αὐτὴν μοιχευθῆναι
καὶ ὃς ἐὰν ἀπολελυμένην
γαμήσῃ μοιχᾶται

But it is said anyone who dismisses his wife
let him give her a certificate of divorce.
But I am saying to you that any divorcing
the wife of him except for the reason of
unfaithfulness makes her commit adultery,
and anyone who a divorced woman
marries commits adultery.

Matthew 5:31-32 · Divorce

My mother told me the mathematics of marriage. It isn't a fifty-fifty deal, but rather it works best when each partner gives seventy-five percent. (Bonnie Clark)

The culture was different in New Testament times. All the power in a marriage resided with the husband and his family, and an unmarried woman had a very difficult life. The book of Ruth offers an example—it tells the story of how hard life was for two widows. Marriage was so much the norm in that culture that the Greek word for "woman" also means "wife," and a single word means both "man" and "husband." For a woman, then, divorce was a very serious matter, depriving her of both status and livelihood.

Verse 31 refers back to Deuteronomy 24:1: "If a man marries a woman who becomes displeasing to him because he finds something indecent about her, and he writes her a certificate of divorce, gives it to her and sends her from his house…." This was a protection for the woman because her husband had to actually give her a document, and couldn't simply throw her out with nothing. Therefore, verse 32 is meant as a new level of protection for a wife. She was not to be sent away unless she had betrayed the marriage vow.

Now, of course, things are different. Each partner has equal say in the marriage and it is no longer a social stigma for a woman to be single or divorced in our society. She is also able to earn a living and enjoy a rich, full life as a single person. Still, these verses teach us that the marriage vow is important and not to be set aside lightly.

One of the keys to understanding this group of verses is respect. Spouses should have respect for each other and for the vows they made. Marriages are meant to be permanent, and though sometimes there is a reason to break them up—such as infidelity or abuse—it is always a sadness. Citizens of the kingdom are not to have the same values as the world, where partners are changed for any minor reason and with the frequency and casualness of buying a new car.

If these verses were meant to protect women of that time, who are the victims of marital breakup today? Children likely suffer most, and for many reasons: instability caused by the divorce; being caught between two parents; economic hardship; being raised without a father or without a mother, or being shuffled back and forth; and having to assume responsibility they were not meant to handle. Human beings grow up best with both parents, and a solid marriage provides a good model to help them if they start a family of their own.

The love talked about in the Bible isn't necessarily romantic love. Romance can come and go and be influenced by outside factors. Rather, a good translation for *agape* is honor or respect. We can give respect to someone whether we have feelings for him or her or not. We can still treat them as human beings. Marriage—like most of life—is not about getting but about giving. Please understand, I do not advocate staying in an abusive marriage or any relationship where there is physical, mental, or emotional danger. But in general, marriage is meant to be a lifelong commitment.

Jesus teaches a new way that runs counter to the way the world thinks and behaves. Love for enemies is radical. Living humbly before God and our fellow humans is radical. Making peace instead of war is radical. Forgiveness is radical. Staying married in a culture that expects the opposite is radical. We are called to a new lifestyle that affects all our relationships—with God and with our fellow human beings.

Expanded translation

> And it was said that anyone who divorces his wife must give her a certificate of divorce. But I am telling you that anyone who dismisses his wife for any reason other than unfaithfulness makes her look like she has committed adultery. And anyone who marries such a woman makes himself look like he is committing adultery. So stop and think how your actions affect others; have respect for your partner and for the promise you made him or her.

8

The Fourth Law
INTEGRITY

πάλιν ἠκούσατε ὅτι ἐρρέθη
τοῖς ἀρχαίοις οὐκ ἐπιορκήσεις
ἀποδώσεις δὲ τῷ κυρίῳ τοὺς ὅρκους σου
ἐγὼ δὲ λέγω ὑμῖν μὴ ὀμόσαι ὅλως

Again you have been taught that it was said
by those of old, "You shall not swear falsely,
but shall fulfill before the Lord your oaths."
But I am telling you, "Do not swear at all."

Matthew 5:33-34a · I Do Solemnly Swear

This verse begins as the others in this section: You have been taught that it was said by your ancestors, "You shall not swear falsely, but shall fulfill your oaths taken before the Lord." There are three different verses this refers to from the Old Testament. The first is Leviticus 19:12, which teaches that swearing falsely while invoking God's name is an affront to God. Numbers 30:2 says that a man must not break a vow he has made to the Lord, and Deuteronomy 23:21 reminds us that vows thus made need to be carried out with dispatch.

This custom of a special standard of truth is also in force today. When someone testifies in a court of law, he or she solemnly swears "to tell the truth, the whole truth, and nothing but the truth." During a marriage ceremony, a bride and groom make vows to each other before God and their witnesses. There are all sorts of special vows, ranging from swearing in a new president to a teenager declaring innocence to a parent: "I never touched the stuff, I swear!"

Does swearing make it true? It should, but people have always been good at weaseling out of things and finding loopholes. Later in Matthew 23:16, Jesus condemns one way of fudging the truth by being very specific by what you swear: "Woe to you, blind guides! You say, 'If anyone swears by the temple, it means nothing; but if anyone swears by the gold of the temple, he is bound by his oath.'"

We can also swear to something just this side of lying: "I promise you, I did not raid the refrigerator for the pie you made for your women's group." (It was already on the counter when I dug into it.) Another example is crossed fingers. When I was a child, crossing one's fingers behind one's back meant the promise made didn't have to be kept.

Though Matthew 5:33 is often translated "break your oath," the more usual translation of the Greek would be to "swear falsely," that is, to give a promise you have no intention of keeping. We all have experience with this; every election we hear campaign promises that will never be kept. The Old Testament is clear—if you make a solemn promise, you need to carry it through.

"But I am telling you," Jesus goes on, "don't swear at all." Quakers and others have taken this verse literally and refused to swear any oaths. This got them into a lot of trouble in the early days and many ended up in prison because they refused to swear to truth in a court of law. Even today, many Quakers will "affirm" in court rather than swear. But there was also a positive side. On June 23, 1683, William Penn signed a friendship treaty with the Lenni-Lenape Indians in Pennsylvania that Voltaire later called "the only treaty never sworn to and never broken."

Why was this important to them? Because swearing assumes a double standard of honesty where you must keep your word in one instance but not in another. This is not the way of the kingdom. Whenever we give our word, others should be able to depend on us. An example of this occurs in *Lord of the Rings: The Two Towers* by J.R.R. Tolkien. The master ring is an instrument of evil that tempts everyone who gets near it with their deepest desires. But one young man, Faramir, has the kind of integrity it takes to deal with even this kind of temptation. He says, "We are truth-speakers, we men of Gondor....*Not if I found it on the highway would I take it* I said. Even if I were such a man as to desire this thing, and even though I knew not clearly what this thing was when I spoke, still I should take those words as a vow, and be held by them."[1]

How many times have we said glibly, "I'll pray for you," and then forgotten all about it—or never really meant to at all? How many times have we said, "I'll think about it," when we really meant "No," but didn't want to come out and say so? How many times have we said "No" to a child, only to give in five minutes later? What does this teach the child? What does this say about our character? Jesus calls us to a higher standard of integrity.

Integrity is more than honesty. Integrity means living your life based on a set of values that permeate all you do. When Jesus talks about the pure of heart in the Beatitudes he means this very thing— having a heart steeped in the values of the kingdom of heaven so that all you say and do springs from that central core. Can we imagine Jesus lying to someone or not carrying through on a promise? Would we require Jesus to put his hand on a Bible before we would believe him? People should be able to trust us, his followers and citizens of the kingdom, just as much. We must take responsibility for our words as much as for our actions. May they always be words for which we proudly take responsibility.

Expanded translation

Furthermore, you have been taught that it was said by your ancestors, "Do not make a promise you don't intend to keep, but fulfill all your solemn vows." But I'm telling you, don't swear at all....

μήτε ἐν τῷ οὐρανῷ ὅτι θρόνος ἐστὶν τοῦ θεοῦ
μήτε ἐν τῇ γῇ ὅτι ὑποπόδιόν ἐστιν
τῶν ποδῶν αὐτοῦ
μήτε εἰς Ἱεροσόλυμα ὅτι
πόλις ἐστὶν τοῦ μεγάλου βασιλέως
μήτε ἐν τῇ κεφαλῇ σου ὀμόσῃς
ὅτι οὐ δύνασαι
μίαν τρίχα λευκὴν ποιῆσαι ἢ μέλαιναν
ἔστω δὲ ὁ λόγος ὑμῶν ναὶ ναί οὒ οὔ
τὸ δὲ περισσὸν τούτων
ἐκ τοῦ πονηροῦ ἐστιν

Not by heaven because it is a throne of God;
not by the earth because it is a footstool
for his feet
not by Jerusalem because
it is the city of the great king;
not by your head swear
because you cannot
one hair white make or black
but let be your word yes, yes, no, no:
for the excess of these
from the evil one is.

Matthew 5:34b-37 · Impertinence, Cheek, Chutzpah, and Other Forms of Irreverence

When we swear, we often swear by something important to show we are sincere. In Old Testament times, people swore by heaven or perhaps the temple. "I swear on my sainted mother's grave" is a modern example. Though there are many reasons not to swear, Jesus mentions one in particular in his admonishment of people who swear by things that don't belong to them and things over which they have no control.

"Don't swear by Jerusalem," Jesus says. It is the city of the great king, and as such we have no right to use it as a witness to an oath. He adds, "Don't swear by your head." We might think a person's body belongs to him or her but, as Jesus reminds us, we don't have as much control as we think—for we are not able to change even the color of our hair by will alone. We can take care of our bodies, but we can't prevent aging, disease, injury, or death.

In our modern world, we have become masters of the excuse:

- "I'm so sorry I forgot" (on purpose).
- "I wanted to come but Mrs. Wilson, who drives the girls to soccer, got sick and I had to fill in." (In fact she had a slight headache and I volunteered.)
- "I had every intention of being there to help but something came up at work." (My coworkers invited me out.)
- "I've been so busy I haven't had time to look in my inbox for a week." (I decided not to check.)

Boil these excuses down and they say one thing: My life and my time are more valuable than yours. In his book *In Praise of Slowness*, Carl Honoré comments, "When people moan 'Oh I'm so busy, I'm run off my feet, my life is a blur, I haven't got time for anything,' what they often mean is, 'look at me; I am hugely important, exciting, and energetic!'"[2] This is not the attitude of a true citizen of the kingdom.

Perhaps rather than invent an excuse, we invent a reason:

- "Oh, I'd love to, but I promised I'd take my mother to the concert that evening." (I'm going home to arrange that right now.)
- "I can't; my cousin from out of town is coming that day." (In fact, he lives in the next town over and we had discussed getting together sometime that week.)

Citizens of the kingdom should not play these word games. Jesus tells us that we should say a simple "yes" or "no." Our speech is to be straightforward, clear, and aboveboard.

This does not mean we simply blurt out whatever is on our mind. There is a difference between truth and lack of control over the tongue. It is never right to lie, but sometimes it is necessary, such as for those who hid Jews in their homes during World War II and lied to the authorities in order to prevent the murder of innocent people.

At the same time, there are many gray areas to truth. Sometimes we stretch it out of kindness: "You look beautiful in the dress" sometimes means as beautiful as that woman can look. We find gray areas in business too. Often we must ask how far we will go to cover for a boss; how justified we are in protecting the company by keeping some or all the truth from a customer; and when we will decide to lie in reverse by not revealing what we know. In a society where those who are honest often lose their jobs, or worse, we must decide when to expose a company's wrongdoing.

A friend of mine once worked in customer service. Occasionally her company made a move that sparked negative comment. On these occasions the customers knew the new policy made little sense and the workers knew as well. Naturally, the employees were forbidden to admit this and were told to give a generic line such as, "The company often tries different ways to reach customers." This explanation was certainly less than the truth and less than honest. Unfortunately, this led to frustration among employees and they began to complain about the customers. Because they were instructed to withhold truth, the workers began to treat their customers with less respect.

Respect, however, should be the motivation behind our words: We tell the truth and we keep our word because we respect ourselves and we respect our brothers and sisters. That's a good rule to use in these gray areas. What I say should show not only that I respect the person I am speaking to but also that I respect myself.

Expanded translation

...not by the universe because it is the throne of God, nor by the ground because it is the stool for God's feet, nor by Jerusalem because it is the city of the great king. Do not swear on your head, either, because you do not have the power in yourself to change even one hair from white to black or back again. If you mean yes, simply say yes, and if you mean no, just say no, for the extra words you add come out of the unregenerate part of your nature—that part that would let you weasel out of a promise.

9

αβγδεζηθικλμνξοπρσστυφχψωαβγδεζηθικλμνξοπρσστυφχψωαβγδεζηθικλμνξοπρσστυφχψω

The Fifth Law

CREATIVE NONVIOLENCE

(Jesus' Third Way)

ἠκούσατε ὅτι ἐρρέθη
ὀφθαλμὸν ἀντὶ ὀφθαλμοῦ καὶ ὀδόντα ἀντὶ ὀδόντος

You have been taught that it was said,
"An eye for and eye and a tooth for a tooth."

Matthew 5:38 · An Eye for an Eye: The Old Testament Standard

As do all the verses in the Sermon on the Mount that point to the Old Testament, this one begins "You have been taught that it was said." This time we have been taught "an eye for an eye and a tooth for a tooth."

The phrase refers back to three passages in the Old Testament: Exodus 21:24, Leviticus 24:19-20, and Deuteronomy 19:21. The Leviticus verses are typical of all three: "If anyone injures his neighbor, whatever he has done must be done to him: fracture for fracture, eye for eye, tooth for tooth. As he has injured the other, so he is to be injured."

Society has tended to look at this verse, especially in modern times, as an unjustified revenge system. As Gandhi said, "An eye for an eye leaves the whole world blind." The Old Testament law, however, originally meant to limit revenge by allowing no more to be done to the perpetrator than had been done to the victim. In actual practice, this often worked out as a monetary compensation. Nor should it be read as encouraging revenge. It is not vengeance, but scrupulous fairness.

Like the verses on divorce that were meant to protect a woman, so these are meant to limit the damage that can be collected. This is a much more merciful law than was found in most of the Middle East at that time, which allowed unlimited revenge for a wrong. Today, in our litigation-happy culture, limiting damages like this could make lawsuits virtually disappear overnight.

Expanded translation

> You have been taught that it was said by those who lived long ago, "An eye to replace an eye, a tooth to replace a tooth, no more."

> ἐγὼ δὲ λέγω ὑμῖν μὴ ἀντιστῆναι
> τῷ πονηρῷ ἀλλ' ὅστις σε ῥαπίζει
> εἰς τὴν δεξιὰν σιαγόνα
> σου στρέψον αὐτῷ καὶ τὴν ἄλλην

> But I am telling you do not set yourself against
> the evil person but if anyone slaps [you]
> on the right cheek
> turn toward him also the other.

Matthew 5:39 · The Infamous "Turn the Other Cheek"

We now move into three verses that have been ill-used in promoting the continuation of injustice, making Christians seem weak and giving nonviolence a bad name through misunderstanding of culture and intent.

Matthew 5:39 begins as many other verses in this section: "But I am telling you...." Jesus' command is that we "do not set [ourselves] up in opposition to an evil person," that is, we do not buy into the situation as set up by this person. Rather than the normal, expected human reaction of retaliation, we are to act instead according to the kingdom values of working toward reconciliation and love, even for the one who hurt us. Notice that although we are not to meet evil with evil, we must not deny that evil exists.

The verb that comes next, *rapazo*, always means "strike with the open hand" or "slap." It is a significant word. Ask someone to cooperate with you, or choose a stuffed animal or a pillow. Try to slap the person or object on the right "cheek," remembering that the Bible assumes everyone is right-handed. The only way it can be done is by backhanding—the kind of blow a superior gives an inferior. The people on the receiving end of injustice in all three of these verses are very much at a disadvantage. Here in 5:39, it is likely a slave. In the next verse, 5:40 we find a very poor person, and in 5:41, a member of a subjugated race.

Another way to take this is demonstrated in the episode "Secrets of the Soul" from the television series *Babylon 5*. A young man, Byron, steps in front of one of his friends who is about to be attacked by another man. "Hit me," Byron instructs, and the attacker does so. "Again." "Again." After the third blow, Bryon looks the man in the eye and asks quietly whether the third blow felt the same as the first or whether there had been any difference between the first, second, and third attacks. The man can only stutter, so Byron continues, "And what would you expect to get out of four, five, and six that you could not get out of one, two, and three?" The man has no answer. Just before leaving with his group, Byron leans close and murmurs, "Your anger has nothing to do with me," and stunned, the man lets them walk away.[1]

Byron demonstrated the principles of nonviolence, or as Walter Wink says, "Jesus' Third Way."[2] In both cases we see the victim:

- Name the evil deed either aloud or by action. We do not name the person evil, but only what he or she is doing.

- Absorb the evil, not allowing it to go any farther. We do not return evil for evil.

- React in a nonviolent, creative way that helps the aggressor see the victim as a person and allows the victim to take back his or her dignity.

- Treat the aggressor as a person, and leave him or her with dignity, freedom of choice, and something to consider.

Remember that in these three verses, Matthew 5:39-41, Jesus is specifically speaking about injustice that is protected by law, such as in the case of masters who have the power of life and death over slaves. Especially in a situation where the law is on the side of the oppressor, it is not our job to force him or her to stop acting unjustly. Force doesn't change one's heart regardless of whether it comes from good or bad intentions. Our job is to prevent the evil from passing unnoticed by not letting it go any further. We also do not reply in kind. Perhaps we may work to pass new laws that are more humane. Our job may be to stand with the victim, or, like Byron, to interpose ourselves between the victim and harm.

Kingdom citizens are not to help perpetuate injustice by silence. Kingdom citizens are not called to be weak. Pacifism is not synonymous with passiveness. Instead, peace calls for courage in the face of evil and injustice, and bold, creative action.

Expanded translation

> But I'm telling you, don't oppose an evil person using the same tactics, but if anybody backhands you, turn so the other cheek is facing. That way, he or she will have to use a fist to hit you again, as an equal.

καὶ τῷ θέλοντί σοι κριθῆναι
καὶ τὸν χιτῶνά σου λαβεῖν ἄφες
αὐτῷ καὶ τὸ ἱμάτιον

And the one wishing you to prosecute
and your tunic to take drop
before him also [your] outer robe.

Matthew 5:40 · Exposing an Unmerciful System

We often think of this illustration from our own cultural context: that is, when someone unjustly takes something from us, we meekly hand over more as well. However, this is a situation where someone rich is taking advantage of someone very poor. If this man is being taken to court for his tunic, it means he has nothing else to his name. The tunic here is a garment worn next to the skin. A person would wear this all the time, for working and for sleeping. According to John's gospel, the Roman soldiers crucifying Jesus divided his outer garment into four pieces but gambled for his tunic.

Here we have a wealthy man, or at least one wealthier than our defendant, who has loaned money that the defendant cannot repay. Rather than feeling pity for this destitute debtor, he hauls him into court in order to force the man to give up his last belongings. Here is a clear case where legality and morality collide and the legal system and the rich win, as so often happens in our world. A modern equivalent might be a bank foreclosing on a farmer after a bad year wipes out all his money. The creditor has a perfect legal right, but the question is whether or not it is moral.

In Old Testament law, according to both Exodus 22:26-27 and Deuteronomy 24:12-13, a creditor was allowed to take a cloak (not a tunic) as security for a debt. He was then to give it back again at sunset, in recognition that the poor debtor needed it to keep warm. According to later Jewish law, if a poor person was not able to repay this debt, it was to be forgiven because of the debtor's poverty.

Therefore, the wealthy person in Matthew 5:40 not only goes against the Torah, but he receives the support of the court system. We have here not just rich versus poor, but a legal system that goes against its own laws and violates its own spirit.

The defendant has lost his case on grounds that are legally and morally shaky. How might he respond?

- He can meekly accept this injustice, bowing to the inevitable and losing his tunic and dignity together.
- He can try to escape, but he's bound to end up right back where he is now in worse trouble than he is in already.
- He can make a speech that nobody will listen to and still lose his tunic.
- He can appeal for mercy, but without expectation of any from either a man who is willing to take his shirt or from an unjust legal system.
- He can get creative and make a statement no one can ignore.

Here he is with only a cloak to cover himself. Instead of slinking away quietly, he drops his cloak, leaving it lying on the floor in a more eloquent statement on the situation than any words could possibly be. As Walter Wink says, he "exposes" the system for what it is. I can picture him looking his creditor and the judge in the eye and then marching out of court in the nude, head held high. "The body is more than clothing, is it not?" Jesus says a little later, and here is a stark example.

Handing his cloak along with his tunic to the wealthy man doesn't change the situation, but it does allow the debtor to meet it on his own terms. If enough people call attention to a bad law it can sometimes change. Perhaps it woke the creditor to what he was doing and softened his heart, even slightly.

This is the most desirable outcome of nonviolent confrontation. It's not about winning; it's about turning someone from evil by changing his or her viewpoint, attitude, and mind. Though it's sometimes nice to wish Bruce Willis or Clint Eastwood would turn up and revenge the oppressor violently, this is not what Jesus teaches. We see a situation in terms of the good person and the bad person, but what God sees are two beloved children, one oppressing the other. It's a scene of sorrow, not of anger, malice, or revenge.

As before, we are to:

- Name the evil action by word or deed.
- Refuse to return evil for evil.
- React in a nonviolent yet creative way to assert our dignity.
- Leave the aggressor with his or her personhood and freedom of choice intact, but with something to consider.

Expanded translation

And for the one wanting to prosecute you to the full extent of the law, even to taking the shirt off your back, expose him and the law for what it is by dropping your coat, too, and leaving it behind you lying on the floor.

καὶ ὅστις σε ἀγγαρεύσει μίλιον ἕν
ὕπαγε μετ' αὐτοῦ δύο

And anyone who will force you mile one
go with him two.

Matthew 5:41 · Going the Extra Mile

In verse 39, we saw a master/slave relationship. Verse 40 addressed the rich and the poor. Here, we look at the conquerors and the subjugated. Again, Jesus deals with a situation that is perfectly legal yet morally questionable and definitely degrading to the victim. As the military overlords of Israel, Roman soldiers had the right to press any Jewish person into temporary service, such as with Simon of Cyrene, who was ordered to carry Jesus' cross when Jesus could not.

The law did have its limits, however: A soldier was only allowed to conscript a conquered person for one Roman mile, close to a modern kilometer. To require someone to go more than this was illegal.

Imagine a Jewish man going about his business when a soldier beckons him over to carry his military paraphernalia. The Jew can't say no—it isn't allowed—so he is forced into the humiliating position of being required to carry the same instruments that help subjugate his people. This is much more than just being inconvenienced because the Jew has no options. He must obey.

We see this on a large scale when an occupying force does whatever it chooses to the citizens of a conquered country. We see it in smaller ways when a worker is forced to do something menial or personal for his or her boss or risk being fired; when a wife must bow to her husband's whims or risk divorce; or when a child lives in a house where his or her parents take advantage of the child's youth. These are situations in which someone with power takes advantage of the powerless in ways that are demeaning but not actually harmful, in ways that cause resentment rather than fear.

There are many ways to creatively challenge unjust laws. The way Jesus mentions here is that, rather than reacting the usual way and sullenly doing as little as possible, we should choose to take charge of the situation by not putting down the pack after one mile. In this way, the Jewish man calls attention to an unjust law and takes back his dignity by acting out of choice. This unexpected action makes the Roman soldier aware of the Jew's humanity. It may even worry him, because the soldier could get into trouble if this were reported. One thing is for sure: The soldier won't forget this quickly. It might even give him pause before he asks the same thing of another. It will not change the Roman Empire or the rules of occupation, but it might change the heart of one soldier.

Throughout history there have been various ways of using nonviolence:

- John Woolman traveled extensively, speaking of the evils of slavery. He didn't refuse to stay with a slave owner, but he paid slaves for their service to him. Eventually his gentle but constant persuasion led Quakers to free all their slaves, long before the American Civil War.

- Susan B. Anthony used her arrest for trying to vote illegally to give her the platform of a very public trial to disseminate her message of equal rights for women.

- In India, Mohandas Gandhi nonviolently protested the British occupation. One of the results of this was a mass protest against the salt tax that helped support British rule. He led thousands to the sea in early 1930 to collect their own salt rather than pay a tax on a product everyone needed.

- In World War II Europe, Corrie Ten Boom's family defied the law quietly by hiding Jews from those who sought to oppress them.

- Rosa Parks pointed out the unfairness of the segregation laws when she refused to give up her bus seat to a white person. The bus driver throwing her off the bus sparked a yearlong bus boycott, which ended segregation on buses in Montgomery, Alabama.

As in these varied cases, in nonviolent resistance we must:

- Name the evil by word or action. Here it is a little different in that the Jewish man is calling attention to the practice by extending it.
- Refuse to return evil for evil.
- React in a nonviolent, creative way to assert our dignity.
- Leave the aggressor with his or her personhood and freedom of choice intact, but with something to consider.

Remember, the purpose of these illustrations is not to applaud the cleverness of the victim, but to encourage us to look at our world and think about creative ways to challenge injustices, especially those we may not have seen because we may have been part of the problem.

Expanded translation

And if anyone will press you into service to carry his pack one mile, go with him two miles. That will take him by surprise, and may make him think!

τῷ αἰτοῦντί σε δός καὶ τὸν
θέλοντα ἀπὸ σοῦ δανίσασθαι μὴ ἀποστραφῇς

To the one asking you, give and the
one wishing from you to borrow do not reject.

Matthew 5:42 · Living Generously

Commentators often overlook this verse because living generously seems out of place between a section on how to react to one's oppressor and a command to love everyone.

Matthew 5:42 refers back to Deuteronomy 15:7-8, about giving liberally to those in need. "If there is a poor man among your brothers in any of the towns of the land that the Lord your God is giving you, do not be hardhearted or tightfisted toward your poor brother. Rather be openhanded and freely lend him whatever he needs." We are to be generous as God is generous, freely giving to all.

The Greek verb *didomi* is in the imperative; it is a command to give to whoever asks. The Greek word for "asking" is more formal than someone wanting a handout; it implies the person asking has a right to expect an answer. As the verses from Deuteronomy make clear, this includes anyone who has a need we can meet.

Perhaps this is Jesus' way of easing his listeners into the "love your enemies" verses. Jesus is focusing on people who are poor and victimized. He says to them, "Don't be afraid to give." A person oppressed knows better than anyone the needs of his or her fellow poor. They need to band together to help one another because all too often no one else is willing.

Two stories from the gospel of Mark are excellent examples of what it means to live generously. Mark 14:3-9 relates the story of a woman who poured nard over Jesus' head, an extravagant act on her part. "Why was the expensive ointment wasted this way?" the men at the table grumble, yet Jesus praised the grand gesture appropriate as an anointing before his burial. At the other end of the spectrum, Mark 12:41-44 tells the story of a poor widow who put two small copper coins into the temple treasury. Jesus commends her highly, for the small amount was more than she could afford. One woman gives the equivalent of a year's wages in expensive ointment, the other only a penny, and yet both are applauded. The message is that both gave out of love and as generously as they could.

I look at these women and ask: How generous have I been with my money, my time, and myself? When I think of my brothers and sisters around the world who have so little in relation to my plenty, I know I have given only out of my abundance, as Jesus observes about the rich at the temple treasury.

True generosity doesn't mean throwing money away and then expecting God to take care of us. But it does mean being alert for needs, seeing and meeting them as best we can. It may mean gathering resources from others so that together we may meet a need. It may also mean going into impoverished areas, to see first-hand the most pressing needs. Generosity also includes being savvy and understanding when resources could be simply wasted. Without a doubt it means more than I am doing right now, and this verse challenges me to live more generously toward my brothers and sisters on this earth.

Expanded translation

Give to anyone who makes a legitimate request of you, and do not reject the one wishing to borrow from you.

10

The Sixth Law
LOVE YOUR ENEMIES

Often the verses of Matthew 5:43 and following are pulled out of context and discussed as a separate piece. But these verses, too, have special meaning in their placement within the sermon.

Jesus has just finished a discourse on creative ways to meet oppression. Human nature makes it easy for us to get carried away by our own cleverness or to think that tricks are okay as long as our target is an oppressor. Jesus' teaching here reminds us that we face fellow human beings, beloved of God. Not every technique is lawful to "bring them down," but only those that leave a person's essential humanity intact. We must always show respect even as we work against oppression.

During an election year in the United States the negative aspects of our human nature become especially noticeable. Watching all the political parties sling accusations back and forth, I mourn the divisions this causes between my fellow citizens. People seem much less concerned about the truth than about proving themselves right, and I do not see anything remotely approaching courtesy or respect in their interactions. I wonder if healing will even be possible after the election, and consider this a prime example of how *not* to treat enemies.

ἠκούσατε ὅτι ἐρρέθη
ἀγαπήσεις τὸν πλησίον σου
καὶ μισήσεις τὸν ἐχθρόν σου

You have been taught that it was said,
"Love your neighbor
and hate your enemy."

Matthew 5:43 · The Old Law

> The command to love my neighbor as I do myself is not an admonition to be nice. It is a statement of truth like the law of gravity.
> (Arthur Waskow)

Matthew 5:43 introduces another section that begins with "You have been taught that it was said." In this case Jesus refers to Leviticus 19:18: "Do not seek revenge or bear a grudge against one of your people, but love your neighbor as yourself. I am the Lord." In this passage it is understood that neighbors are fellow chosen ones of God. Jesus' audience would have agreed absolutely. We are to love those in our group and hate those who are outsiders.

This is still a popular sentiment today. We are likely to respect anything said by our own gurus and dismiss statements from the other side as the lies of good-for-nothing scoundrels. In my part of the world, the Caucasian population often makes fun of Hispanics and Native Americans. In other places subjects of scorn may include Puerto Ricans, Africans, Asians, gays, teenagers, or senior citizens. Religions are especially good at vilifying others as evidenced in the age-old struggle between Christians, Muslims, and Jews. In the Christian community alone Catholics and Protestants have plenty to say about each other as do fundamentalists and liberals. Humans are exceptionally good at erecting fences and then looking down on those on the other side.

In a folktale, two farmers named Joe and Mike quarrel over a piece of land. Mike diverts the stream and forms a new creek, dividing their property. Joe decides to go one step further and build a wall, and he hires a carpenter to do the work. But when Joe comes back to check that evening, he sees that the carpenter built a bridge instead. Before Joe becomes furious, Mike crosses the bridge with tears in his eyes. "Thank you for caring enough to build a bridge to me," he says, and their friendship is restored. Although Joe's reconciliation was somewhat unintentional, God intentionally builds bridges to us and we should intentionally build bridges to others.

During New Testament times, Middle Eastern societies were built on honor. When we hear the word *agape* or *love* today, we tend to think of the emotional aspect. For Jesus' hearers, however, *agape* meant "honor"; and *echthros*, which we translate as "hate," meant "shun," or "to show no honor." Honor was as important in Jesus' time as respect is today. To honor at that time was to treat someone with the esteem you would show your own family—the esteem you expected to be shown to you. For instance, a host would honor a stranger by welcoming him or her in, offering food and drink and a place to sleep, and—in the Greek world, at least—sending the guest on with gifts to help in the continuing journey. This perspective adds a whole new richness of meaning to verses like John 3:16: This is how God showed honor to the world—God sent the only son, with terms so generous we only have to believe to be forgiven our rebellion and be accepted into God's family.

Expanded translation

You have heard that it was said you shall give honor to your neighbor and shun the one dishonoring you.

ἐγὼ δὲ λέγω ὑμῖν ἀγαπᾶτε τοὺς ἐχθροὺς ὑμῶν
καὶ προσεύχεσθε ὑπὲρ τῶν διωκόντων ὑμᾶς

But I am telling you love your enemies
and pray on behalf of the ones harassing you.

Matthew 5:44 · The New Law—Love Your Enemies

This verse, like others, begins "But I am telling you." This time Jesus makes the outrageous demand, "Love your enemies, and pray for those who persecute you." As citizens of the kingdom, we are not only to respect our enemies, but pray for those who harass us. This is perhaps impossible apart from God.

The enemies of Jesus' first-century hearers were clearly the Romans who had invaded their country. It may not be as easy to decide who our enemies are today, though for some, naming personal enemies is not difficult. Modern enemies might include a coworker, a boss, a relative, a neighbor, or a stranger who wishes us ill. Being around someone who doesn't wish you well is not an easy experience.

It can also be difficult to name enemies of the church in modern times. I know people who would quickly list atheists, the American Civil Liberties Union, gays, secular humanists, or liberals. Others would include fundamentalists just as quickly. Some would say the media or name those of a different country, a different religion, or a different denomination. Others would mention the people within the church itself who live according to values other than those of the sermon. Do we consider the enemies of our nation to be the enemies of our church as well? Defining our enemy is very important because the one we call our enemy in many ways defines who we are and where we come from. Whom we call enemy may say more about us than about those we perceive as against us.

Perhaps in order to clarify this verse we must ask about the enemies of Jesus. They weren't the occupying forces of Israel; Jesus and the Romans managed to steer clear of one another until the end of Jesus' life when the Romans were forced to intervene. Jesus' enemies weren't the "sinners"—the downtrodden, the poor, the ill, the disenfranchised—who flocked to hear him. Instead, Jesus' enemies were the religious establishment of his day; highly moral, smug, self-satisfied, self-righteous, judgmental people; people with a vested interest in the status quo and in keeping their positions and their privileges; and people who put their national interests ahead of the love, compassion, forgiveness, and mercy of God. Unfortunately, people today fit these descriptions too.

What does it mean to love the enemies of our country? At the very least, it means remembering that they are people. Think of all the nicknames given to the other side in wars: huns, Krauts, Japs, rag heads, and gooks, to name a few. Nicknames serve to depersonalize the enemy; it is so much easier to hate and justify killing a gook, for instance, than a fellow human being. It is much easier to kill a terrorist than a fellow human being. It is easier to kill a fanatic. But if we really believe all human beings are beloved children of God, we might be more willing to sit down, listen, and find common ground. It certainly won't be easy, however, for making peace is always more difficult than waging war.

The second half of Matthew 5:44 reminds us to pray for those harassing us. The word for "pray" is formed from two simpler words, *pros*, meaning "for the benefit of," and *euchomai*, "to make requests of God." How do we pray for the benefit of those who do not wish us well? We read examples in Scripture of both Jesus and Stephen praying for those who were killing them, that the sin not be laid to their murderers' accounts. Though we seldom meet anything so drastic today—at least not in America—it is still hard to pray for the benefit of one who hurts our child at school, wins through underhanded tactics a promotion we deserved, spreads lies about our family, or insults us deeply. To forgive these injustices is hard enough, but to actually pray for the person's benefit is something we simply can't do on our own. Logic breaks down here, and we realize that God sees the world very differently than we do.

In order to obey, we must not forget that God died for those who hurt us and loves them very much. We must curb our natural human reaction to hate or strike back. Second, we must remember that God sees all that happens and can turn even the worst circumstances to good. Last, we must remember that what God thinks of us is what matters, not what anyone else thinks. Extending grace to those who do not wish us well is both the heart of the kingdom message and the hardest thing asked of us.

Expanded translation

> But I'm telling you, love and honor your enemies and those who dishonor you, and pray on behalf of those who harass you…

ὅπως γένησθε
υἱοὶ τοῦ πατρὸς ὑμῶν τοῦ ἐν οὐρανοῖς
ὅτι τὸν ἥλιον αὐτοῦ ἀνατέλλει ἐπὶ πονηροὺς
καὶ ἀγαθοὺς καὶ βρέχει ἐπὶ
δικαίους καὶ ἀδίκους

In order that you will turn out to be
[genuine] children of your Father in the heavens,
because his sun he causes to rise upon evil [people]
and good [people] and sends rain upon
righteous [people] and unrighteous [people].

Matthew 5:45 · Of Sun and Rain

This verse fills me with wonder and provides a window into the wideness of God's mercy. The hymn "How Great Thou Art" begins "Oh Lord my God! When I in awesome wonder/Consider all the worlds Thy hands have made...."[1] The psalmist says: "When I consider your heavens, the work of your fingers, the moon and the stars, which you have set in place, what is man that you are mindful of him, the son of man that you care for him? You made him a little lower than the heavenly beings and crowned him with glory and honor" (Psalm 8:3-5). Or as God demanded of Job: "Where were you when I laid the earth's foundation? Tell me, if you understand. Who marked off its dimensions? Surely you know! Who stretched a measuring line across it?" (Job 38:4-5). God the Creator, God the Almighty, is also God the Generous.

I think of the beauty of the earth: the majestic mountains, the rushing mountain streams, the blue lakes, emerald forests, the mighty oceans. Looking up at night I see the incredible vista of the Milky Way, the stars and planets, and the moon and meteors in an amazing celestial display. During the day the sun warms me. God sends spring, summer, fall, and winter to grow crops to feed us. Abundance and beauty surround us.

God the Almighty promises to meet our needs, but we receive so much more than our needs in the abundance of plants, animals, natural beauty, and the cycles of nature. We have done nothing to deserve God's generosity.

Nor does God require allegiance before bestowing these wonderful gifts. The sun warms us and grows our crops. The rain falls on the fields of the righteous farmer and on the fields of the unrighteous. Imagine what would happen if people had to swear allegiance to God before getting what they needed to live. We would have a rash of fear-induced conversions. But God gives first, and gives again and again, waiting patiently for our response. God shows love for all humanity in every sunrise, dawning not only on the Mother Teresas, but on the Saddam Husseins; not only on Caucasians, but on every person of every race; and on the moral, the immoral, and everyone in between. We haven't yet begun to realize the depth of God's mercy and generosity. It is awe-inspiring in the truest sense.

Jesus says that God's children should show the family likeness. We love our enemies because we want to be like our heavenly Parent, who loves and cares for all people. When we think of all God does for all of us, showing compassion toward someone who is harassing us doesn't seem like much to ask. Indeed, if we are to be true members of God's family, we must begin seeing others with the same love with which our heavenly Parent sees.

Expanded translation

> ...in order that you will turn out to be [genuine] children of your heavenly Parent; because God causes God's sun to rise on the wicked and the good and sends rain upon both those who practice justice toward others and those who are unjust in their dealings.

ἐὰν γὰρ ἀγαπήσητε τοὺς ἀγαπῶντας ὑμᾶς
τίνα μισθὸν ἔχετε
οὐχὶ καὶ οἱ τελῶναι τὸ αὐτὸ ποιοῦσιν
καὶ ἐὰν ἀσπάσησθε τοὺς ἀδελφοὺς ὑμῶν μόνον
τί περισσὸν ποιεῖτε
οὐχὶ καὶ οἱ ἐθνικοὶ τὸ αὐτὸ ποιοῦσιν

For if you love the ones loving you,
what reward do you have?
Do not even the tax collectors the same do?
And if welcome the friends of you only
what remarkable [thing] have you done?
Do not even the Gentiles the same do?

Matthew 5:46-47 · God Doesn't Grade on the Curve

Many of us know someone who scrupulously keeps track and pays in kind—the same value of Christmas present, a dinner for a dinner, and favor for a favor. If we do more or less for this person it flusters that person and his or her sense of fairness.

Many of us keep birthday lists of who gets a present from us because they gave one, and who just gets a card. The same is true for our Christmas lists. Some people get presents, some get personal letters, and some get a simple signed card. Then there are those who serve us. My mother always sent a present for my teacher and always gave the newspaper carrier a little extra money. As a rule, most people give when they know they will receive and give in appreciation of services rendered. Some give to their church with the attitude of helping an institution that helps them, rather than give to express gratitude to God. Alumni now ask colleges what the school can do for them rather than give back to their alma maters in appreciation of the education they received.

Reciprocal giving is fine, but for Jesus it marks the lowest common denominator. "What kind of reward do you expect for this?" he asks. Choirs of angels singing for you? Your name up in lights? Citation as an example in the next church newsletter? Unfortunately, God isn't passing out rewards for the easy stuff.

"Even the tax collectors do the same." Tax collectors were a despised bunch who not only worked for the Roman occupation force, but also got rich at the expense of their fellow Jews. It's not hard to think of those today who make obscene profits from their products and who rip off taxpayers and consumers. Even these people give generously where it does them good—where it gets them good publicity, strokes their ego, or gives them tax breaks or other help from elected officials. If we give only to our friends and to those who will give to us, we are no better.

There was a push a few years ago prompting the public to do random acts of kindness such as paying the toll for the car behind us or giving flowers to a stranger. Some grumbled that we should instead be thinking out our generosity to give where it was most needed, as indeed we should. But sprinkling random acts of kindness in our daily lives is very much in the spirit of the sermon.

One reason to be generous is that generosity counteracts our tendency to worship money, to treat financial gain as something serious, something to hoard. We treat money as something that belongs to us and generally we spend it on whatever we please, for ourselves. However, as Philip Yancey reminds us in *Rumors of Another World*, Jesus' attitude toward money can be summed up in the phrase, "You can't take it with you."[2] We need to learn to hold our money lightly and set it free to do good in the world.

Verse 47 adds to verse 46. If we show honor only to those who are our friends and associates and only to those who belong to our circle, class, church, political party, race—to anyone who is enough like us to matter—what have we done that's so remarkable? Everybody does that; it's a human characteristic.

Jesus instructs us to meet people at a deeper level than the group to which they belong, whether that's religion, gender, race, economic class, or political persuasion. We are to meet others at the place of their personhood where soul can talk to soul. People are more than their jobs, more than their racial/social/sexual/gender identity, and even more than the face they present to the outside world. In *Synchronicity*, Joseph Jaworski suggests we begin the process of connecting by meeting people's eyes.[3] Even this is not as easy as it sounds.

We need to move past the realm of reciprocal giving and into generosity toward those who can't pay us back and who can't offer us a reward. This is not solely about money but also about time. More importantly, this is about respect and seeing those who are not of our group as beloved children of God.

This respectful attitude is first postulated in verse 45 with God's remarkable generosity and love toward us. Jesus should be our example in the way he gave both aid and respect to everyone he met. I plan to take what I normally spend on Christmas presents for my family and use that money to help those in need. I have invited my family to do the same and to give to a cause in which they believe instead of sending me a present. There are many ways to creatively give time and money to those who can't repay. Make meals, offer a ride, listen, visit a nursing home, pay a bill, clean, mow a lawn, donate a phone card—the list is endless. The needs are great both at home and abroad.

Expanded translation

> For if you are nice only to the people who are nice to you, do you expect a reward? Even the rich, who will cheat practically anyone, do that much. And if you welcome only your friends or those of your own social class, what have you done that's so remarkable? Even those you consider outside God's love and provision do exactly the same thing.

ἔσεσθε οὖν ὑμεῖς τέλειοι
ὡς ὁ πατὴρ ὑμῶν ὁ οὐράνιος τέλειός ἐστιν

You be therefore perfect
as your heavenly Father perfect is.

Matthew 5:48 · Grow Up!

Note that this verse begins with a *therefore,* pointing back not only to all that Jesus has said so far but specifically to the previous verses in which he calls us to respect all people and to live generously. This verse also contains the controversial phrase: "be perfect." If Jesus knew he was talking to fallible human beings, why would he command the impossible?

When I was young, my religious tradition taught that we could be perfect here on earth and reach a point where we no longer sinned. There was one big drawback to this: Once a person declared he or she had reached that place—and it was expected that the spiritually serious would do so—he or she could no longer admit any missteps. Though many sincere people lived good lives, there was also a temptation for "evangelical Phariseeism" in which a person talked and acted one way at church and lived another way in private. As we shall see in Matthew 6, Jesus reserves his harshest words for people like these.

The word translated "perfect" is from the Greek *teleios,* a word that indicates such qualities as full-grown, fulfilled, mature, and adult. Jesus calls us to act like adults in the midst of a selfish, childish world. It is impossible to imagine Jesus pouting or acting spitefully because he didn't get his own way. He modeled the very epitome of mature, adult behavior, and calls us to follow that path.

This verse is the very heart of the sermon. The word from Jesus is to "Act like adults," or even more simply, "Grow up!" Though we are to be childlike in our faith, we are to be adult in our relationships.

Another facet of "growing up" is that we are to grow into the people we are meant to be. I don't have to be Mother Teresa, St. Paul, or anybody else. I am called to grow truly into Karen Oberst and fulfill the destiny to which God calls me, the destiny that is mine alone, and the work that will not get done if I don't do it.

Expanded translation

> Grow up! Start acting the part of mature adults. As your heavenly Parent is grace-full and generous toward all those who dwell on earth, so you should follow God's example and act with grace and generosity toward your fellow human beings.

11

αβγδεζηθικλμνξοπρςστυφχψωαβγδεζηθικλμνξοπρςστυφχψωαβγδεζηθικλμνξοπρςστυφχψω

REACHING OUT TO OTHERS

Matthew 5 ends with Jesus' admonition to act as adults. Matthew 6 fleshes out that statement with some examples of mature and not-so-mature behavior. This middle chapter of the Sermon on the Mount serves as a how-to guide in which Jesus gives us practical advice about:

- Giving to others
- Praying
- Fasting
- Handling money and possessions

Jesus speaks out against those who perform religious actions for the wrong reasons—a topic that begins in Matthew 6 and continues into Matthew 7. As we saw in Matthew 5, attitude comes first and actions follow. People still trying to impress others are not yet living kingdom lives.

In this first section of Matthew 6, Jesus discusses how to live our lives in connection with other people. He has already talked about living a generous and grace-full life, and the issue here is how we do it. Again, as throughout the sermon, our attitude is vital. We must reach out to meet needs from a grateful heart, acting as God's hands and feet to our fellow human beings.

προσέχετε δὲ τὴν δικαιοσύνην ὑμῶν
μὴ ποιεῖν ἔμπροσθεν τῶν ἀνθρώπων πρὸς
τὸ θεαθῆναι αὐτοῖς εἰ δὲ μή γε μισθὸν οὐκ
ἔχετε παρὰ τῷ πατρὶ ὑμῶν τῷ ἐν τοῖς οὐρανοῖς.

But take care your righteousness
not to do before people in order
to be seen by them otherwise a reward you do not
have from your Father in heaven.

Matthew 6:1 · Who Are You Trying to Impress?

We all like to be appreciated. When we do something nice for someone and he or she doesn't notice or acknowledge it, we hurt. Even those who prefer to work behind the scenes want to be noticed occasionally. Jesus understands our human nature, and in the last part of Matthew 5, we learned about following God's lead in being grace-full and generous. We take this to heart and reach out to others, but if we aren't careful, we begin to feel special and superior and want everybody else to be aware of our kindness. We want to be petted and praised. Though we desire appreciation and acknowledgement, our self-importance has no place in the nature of a citizen of the kingdom of heaven. In fact, Jesus is quite emphatic.

The beginning of Matthew 6:1 is usually translated as "Be careful." However, the Greek construction indicates something stronger such as, "Pay attention!" or "Watch!"

Does this mean that if somebody notices we have done something good, it negates our reward in heaven? Lloyd C. Douglas postulates this viewpoint in his novel *Doctor Hudson's Secret Journal*.[1] Dr. Hudson does hundreds of acts of charity, but always gives people strict instructions not to tell anyone else. It is only after he dies that his family and friends hear from the scores of people he has helped and realize what an incredibly generous man he was. Dr. Hudson's life modeled the command to give in secret as expressed in Matthew 6:1-4. Jesus often requested people keep the things he did for them a secret. Secrecy can be a good rule to follow because it promotes humility, one of the key kingdom virtues. At the same time, this verse isn't meant to be a threat or a warning. The underlying point is that we must live lifestyles exemplifying kingdom values out of gratitude for what God has done for us regardless of whether or not anyone notices.

This verse is often considered part of the next three verses about giving. The New International Version, for instance, pulls Matthew 6:1-4 together under the heading "Giving to the Needy" while *The Message* uses "The World is Not a Stage." The King James Version translates the word *dikaiosumen* as "alms" rather than "righteousness" in order to fit in with what follows. However, the verse is more like an introduction to the next section. *Dikaiosumen* covers the whole range of inward righteousness, outward justice, our inward change of attitude, and the outward acts that result. Jesus reached out to people out of compassion and we are to do likewise.

We might be called to live our lives publicly, like Jesus or Mother Teresa, but more likely, we will offer small acts of compassion that no one but the recipient ever knows about. As always, attitude is the key. Let us listen to God telling us which needs are our responsibility to meet—whether those are the needs of the people we see every day or the needs of those across the world.

Expanded translation

> But be careful! Don't adopt the kingdom lifestyle for the express purpose of impressing people; if you do, you do not have any reward from your heavenly Parent.

ὅταν οὖν ποιῇς ἐλεημοσύνην
μὴ σαλπίσῃς ἔμπροσθέν σου
ὥσπερ οἱ ὑποκριταὶ ποιοῦσιν ἐν ταῖς συναγωγαῖς
καὶ ἐν ταῖς ῥύμαις ὅπως δοξασθῶσιν
ὑπὸ τῶν ἀνθρώπων ἀμὴν λέγω ὑμῖν
ἀπέχουσιν τὸν μισθὸν αὐτῶν

When therefore you do charitable deeds
do not sound a trumpet before you
as the hypocrites do in the synagogues
and in the streets so that they may be praised
by people. Truly I say to you
they have received in full their reward.

Matthew 6:2 · "I'm Not Really a Kingdom Subject; I Just Play One on the Stage"

Hypocrites are bothersome. In fact, they often call forth loathing in us as few other people do. We can all think of individuals who:

- Mouth pious platitudes about helping children while cutting money for programs to assist them. Their words sound good, but nothing gets done.

- Speak so movingly on Sunday of how following Christ has changed their life but during the week sell shoddy merchandise at inflated prices. They do not live out values of integrity and honesty.

- Are sweet and understanding to our face but speak against us behind our back. This not only shows a lack of respect, but goes against the teaching of simple and honest speech.

In "A Letter from Birmingham Jail," Martin Luther King, Jr., writes about the hypocrisy of white Christians who already have respect and opportunities and yet tell their black brothers and sisters they must wait for theirs. "While confined here in the Birmingham city jail, I came across your recent statement calling my present activities 'unwise and untimely'....You deplore the demonstrations that are presently taking place in Birmingham. But your statement, I am sorry to say, fails to express a similar concern for the conditions that brought about the demonstrations."[2]

I once met a woman who was highly skilled but, being desperate for work in a poor economic climate, took a position far below her abilities. Because she was in this lower position, she was constantly treated like a second-class worker. Every time she offered to do more she was rebuffed and told to keep her place. Yet when she finally found a better job and prepared to leave, she was suddenly everybody's friend. The same people who had treated her so shabbily were now praising her skills and talking about how happy they were for her. And bless her heart, she was so gracious that she never said any of the things she might have said.

The Greek word comes to us almost directly: *hupokrites*. It had a slightly different meaning back in the first century; it was the word for an actor on the stage pretending to be somebody else. What Jesus describes here is the first-century equivalent of a photo opportunity. A wealthy person heads into the poorer part of town. We know it is poor because the word Jesus uses for "street" means "narrow," as opposed to referring to the broad main thoroughfare. This wealthy person then hires someone to go before him, blowing a trumpet so everyone can see him doing a work of charity. What a vivid picture! The wealthy person marches in and makes a big production about handing out a few coins to the poor while everyone murmurs, "What a great and generous man!" Think of how the poor must feel having their needs humiliatingly exposed by the same people who exploit them.

Even today, a wealthy donor gives money to a college to get his name on a building. A celebrity takes a few minutes out of a busy schedule to be photographed with poor children. A company gives a large donation of money or equipment both as a tax write-off and for publicity.

I've worked for several colleges and I have seen that donors are nearly always treated the same. Those who give lots of money, or who might potentially give lots of money, are treated like royalty, escorted around the campus, given dinners, and written up in the school newsletter. The thousands of alumni who give smaller gifts year after year are often overlooked, missing out on the opportunities given the wealthy.

The word translated "receive," *apecho*, is an interesting one. Originally it meant "to keep off" or "to keep away from." By New Testament times it became a commercial term written across the bottom of documents to mean "paid in full." Those who give to others for the publicity or the good feelings it gives them have already been paid in full. They might impress people, but they won't impress God.

We get a slightly different viewpoint in Luke 21:1-4. In this situation, rich people are putting large offerings into the temple treasury. A poor widow giving only two small coins follows them. Jesus commends the widow for giving far more than the others because the two coins represent a much larger percentage of her money. In the very next chapter of Luke, Jesus is betrayed and arrested; this word about prideful giving is one of his very last teachings to his disciples. If Jesus felt it such an important concept to point out at a time like that, perhaps we should give it some thought.

It is clear that generosity is judged very differently in the kingdom. May we learn to give and to do for others out of love and generosity and in order to please only our heavenly Parent.

Expanded translation

> When you do something for somebody because they need it, don't make a dramatic production out of it, choose rush hour for your "kindnesses," or play to the admiring crowd as some do. I can assure you their invoice is already marked "paid in full" and there is nothing else due them.

σοῦ δὲ ποιοῦντος ἐλεημοσύνην
μὴ γνώτω ἡ ἀριστερά σου
τί ποιεῖ ἡ δεξιά σου
ὅπως ᾖ σου ἡ ἐλεημοσύνη ἐν τῷ κρυπτῷ
καὶ ὁ πατήρ σου ὁ βλέπων ἐν τῷ κρυπτῷ
ἀποδώσει σοι

But you performing charitable acts
not know your left hand
what is doing your right hand
so that your charitable acts are [done] in secret.
And your Father observing in secret
will reward you.

Matthew 6:3-4 · Stealth Giving

Jesus says that when we perform our acts of compassion, we should be so quiet that our left hand hardly realizes what our right hand is doing.

Eleemosune, often translated "give," implies more than giving money. Its base meaning is "merciful, compassionate," and the word includes any act done for someone who needs help—gifts of time, money, or attention, for example. Much more than one particular act, it implies a lifestyle. When we see a need, we give because that's what kingdom citizens do. Paul gives us a lovely description of this sort of lifestyle in Colossians 3:12: "Therefore, as God's chosen people, holy and dearly loved, clothe yourselves with compassion, kindness, humility, gentleness and patience." To that list, Jesus would add generosity.

Why does Jesus command us to do our good deeds secretly? As I have mentioned before, secrecy fosters humility in the giver, one of the prime characteristics of a kingdom citizen. We must not give to be noticed, we must give because there's a need. Some of my happiest memories are of times I have given without anyone but God noticing, sometimes so secretly and deftly that the recipient never discovered it was me. At the same time, this does not excuse us from acknowledging the work of others. We all know many people who do things to make our life easier, and though it is true that we don't serve in order to be noticed and praised, we are not excused from being grateful to others.

Another reason we are to give secretly is to maintain the self-respect of the person in need. We don't want to make a situation worse by throwing a spotlight on another's needs or failures. Forcing someone into a victim role in public is unkind, especially concerning needs that can be met privately. Some needs do need to be made generally known, such as the lack of justice faced by whole groups of people. In cases where the powerful exploit the disenfranchised, it is time to speak the truth to power and call for change. When helping individuals, however, we must act quietly and search for the appropriate response whether that's giving money, listening, offering to help in some way, or just speaking a kind word. We must serve according to our gifts to meet the needs we see.

The last part of verse 4 can be taken several ways: First, our heavenly Parent may be watching what we are doing from a hidden, secret place; second, God may be seeing what *we* do in secret. (This verse is most often translated this second way.) The third way is perhaps the most interesting: The heavenly Parent, who also works in secret, sees what you are doing. This certainly goes along with the God of Matthew 5 who sends us what we need to live, not requiring acknowledgement from anyone nor making a big fanfare. In this last case, by acting in secret we display our family characteristics. The Greek doesn't favor one of these explanations over the others and all lend themselves to interesting conclusions.

The word for "reward," *apodidomai*, conveys the sense that a person is rewarded for his or her contributions at work through a paycheck; it's more of a reimbursement than what we would call a reward today. If a person helps others merely to impress the right people, then this is his or her reward. There's a line in the movie *An American Christmas Carol* spoken by the Scrooge character Ben Slade: "Never pay a man one penny more than he's worth."[3] If, on the other hand, we meet a need quietly, simply to help a brother or sister, we leave the payment up to God, who pays us much more than we are worth.

One final note: The King James Version adds *openly*—that is, if we perform our good deeds in secret, God will reward us openly. Most versions of the Greek don't include this, however, and it is likely a late addition.

Expanded translation

> When you are helping someone in need, do it secretly and quietly so that your left hand hardly realizes what your right hand is doing. Your heavenly Parent, who also works behind the scenes, sees what you are doing and will take care of your reimbursement.

12

TEACHING ON PRAYER

καὶ ὅταν προσεύχησθε οὐκ ἔσεσθε ὡς
οἱ ὑποκριταί ὅτι φιλοῦσιν
ἐν ταῖς συναγωγαῖς καὶ ἐν ταῖς γωνίαις
τῶν πλατειῶν ἑστῶτες προσεύχεσθαι
ὅπως φανῶσιν τοῖς ἀνθρώποις
ἀμὴν λέγω ὑμῖν ἀπέχουσιν
τὸν μισθὸν αὐτῶν σὺ δὲ ὅταν προσεύχῃ
εἴσελθε εἰς τὸ ταμεῖόν σου καὶ
κλείσας τὴν θύραν σου πρόσευξαι τῷ πατρί σου
τῷ ἐν τῷ κρυπτῷ
καὶ ὁ πατήρ σου ὁ βλέπων ἐν τῷ κρυπτῷ
ἀποδώσει σοι

And when you pray do not be like
the hypocrites because they love
in the synagogues and on the corners
of the broad streets standing to pray,
in order to be seen by men.

> Truly I say to you they have
> their reward. But you when you pray,
> enter into your inner room and
> closing your door pray to your Father
> in the secret place;
> and your Father observing in secret
> will reward you.

Matthew 6:5-6 · Praying to the Audience

Here are our old friends, the play actors, practicing their religion to an admiring crowd. This time they are praying, and not in the poor part of town. This time they are standing on the corners of the wide streets. We can guess the contents of their prayers from the parable of the Pharisee and the tax collector in Luke 18:9-14: "The Pharisee stood up and prayed about himself: 'God, I thank you that I am not like other men—robbers, evildoers, adulterers—or even like this tax collector. I fast twice a week and give a tenth of all I get.'" The Pharisee invokes God's name only as a prelude to naming his own virtues and congratulating himself on his righteousness.

The word translated "pray," *proseuchomai*, is not as narrow as the way we use the word *pray* today. Instead, *proseuchomai* encompasses all of worship. Often we show up at church out of habit, because it's expected, because it makes us feel good, or because it makes good business sense for our customers to see us in church. We know the right words, we know how to act, and we even know the right facial expressions.

A kingdom citizen doesn't gather with other believers to impress anyone or keep up appearances, but instead gathers because public worship is such a precious time of seeking God in community. The church I attend isn't perfect, but when we meet Sunday morning, we do all our chatting and catching up on each other's lives in the narthex, the entryway of the church. Once we walk through the doors into the sanctuary, our focus is on God. The first time I attended there I was awed by the sense of God's Spirit in that place.

Once a month we have an unprogrammed meeting without singing or preaching. Instead, we sit together in a silence broken only by the words God gives us to speak. This kind of worship—seeking God alone and yet in community—is powerful. In many ways it is the antithesis of the play actor Jesus describes in Matthew 6:5-6. Public worship should be done with its focus on God, not on those who may see us with our heads bowed.

Interestingly, this passage begins with public worship and then moves to private worship. Often what we learn from worshiping together can enrich our private worship in the coming week.

In discussing private worship, Jesus instructs us to go into an inner room to pray—a room free from distractions and not visible from the streets. This is not necessarily literal; we can find places to pray anywhere. I have a special chair where I sit with a cup of tea to pray and meditate. Some people find that place outdoors. What is important is that the place we choose be free from distractions. We meet our Lord there in quiet, with no one to impress. We let pretensions drop away and we pray. We pray by speaking and by listening; forms are not important. Later in Matthew 6, Jesus will give us a pattern for our prayers, but following each step every day isn't necessary, either. God's grace to us is liberty. When we appear before God in honesty, humility, and trust, God speaks to us and directs our life.

So here's the word from Jesus: When you worship publicly, make sure your focus is on God and not on those around you. When you worship privately, go to a place without distractions where you can be honest before God and listen to what God has to say.

I know this may not be possible every day or in certain situations, such as when raising young children. We can be thankful that God understands when we can't carve out a long, quiet stretch of time to pray. However, we can train ourselves to be alert for God even in the busiest times of life, as Brother Lawrence describes in *The*

Practice of the Presence of God. Despite laboring many hours each day as a cook in a large monastery, Brother Lawrence worked to make prayer a constant dialogue. Prayer and worship are the food and drink of the kingdom citizen. We neglect them at our peril.

Expanded translation

> When you worship, don't put on a show for the crowd as the playactors do. Believe me when I say their account has been marked "paid in full." But whenever you pray, enter into your inner room (which is private and cannot be seen from the street), and having barred your door, pray to your heavenly Parent in the secret place. And your Parent, who likewise works in secret, will reward you.

> προσευχόμενοι δὲ μὴ βατταλογήσητε ὥσπερ
> οἱ ἐθνικοί δοκοῦσιν γὰρ ὅτι ἐν τῇ
> πολυλογίᾳ αὐτῶν εἰσακουσθήσονται
> μὴ οὖν ὁμοιωθῆτε αὐτοῖς
> οἶδεν γὰρ ὁ πατὴρ ὑμῶν ὧν
> χρείαν ἔχετε πρὸ τοῦ ὑμᾶς αἰτῆσαι αὐτόν
>
> ---
>
> But praying do not babble as
> the Gentiles, for they believe in their
> many words they shall be heard.
> Do not be like them,
> understands for your Father what
> you have need of before you ask him.

Matthew 6:7-8 · Simple, Honest Prayer

When the solution is simple, God is answering. (Albert Einstein)

When Jesus talks about our speaking he reminds us repeatedly that simple is beautiful. In Matthew 5:37, for instance, he instructs us to say just "yes" or "no" without adding anything else. Here he reminds us that adding a lot of words to our prayers simply isn't necessary.

The Greek word *battalogésete*, translated "vain repetitions," "babbling," "ramble," and "meaningless repetitions" is a little hard to translate precisely because in the New Testament it appears only here and in the sermon's parallel passage—Luke 11:2. The root meaning in older Greek is "to stutter." Many of us know people who offer beautiful, elaborate, properly phrased, long prayers in church. These vary from the pious, flowery prayers of evangelical or fundamental churches to the elaborately structured prayers in the liturgical tradition. They can be beautiful and meaningful when offered sincerely, but if these prayers don't come from the heart, they become just so much stammering. This comes as good news to someone like me who never did get the hang of either the God language or the proper intonations of those prayers.

There are a good, practical reasons for Jesus' warning in this verse. First, elaborate prayer can build a barrier between a worshiper and God. Those who worship often believe they will be heard because of their "much-speaking," such as in the story of Elijah and the prophets of Baal (1 Kings 18:17-40). In a challenge to the prophets of Baal, Elijah proposes a test. The prophets of Baal will prepare a sacrifice, and Elijah will prepare a sacrifice of his own. The god who answers with fire from heaven to consume the sacrificed animals will be considered the true God. The prophets of Baal first call on their gods, then dance around their altar, and finally cut themselves until blood runs, all to no avail. Elijah, on the other hand, prays one simple prayer to God and God answers promptly.

In the New Testament version, a Pharisee prays his fancy, elaborate prayer at the same time a tax collector prays simply, "God, have mercy on me, a sinner." Jesus says that it is the tax collector's prayer that God answers. When we hear prayers in flowery language or prayers clothed in ritual, it is possible to get carried away by the beauty of the prayer and forget the very God to whom they are addressed. Ritual can also cloak God in mystery and awe to the point that we don't feel worthy to approach God on our own.

Although ritual or beautifully worded prayers can help get us into a proper frame of mind to worship, silence can serve the same purpose. Quakers call this "centering down." Regardless, we must never confuse our feelings with reality nor let them isolate us from the living God. We worship the God who created the universe; answered Elijah with fire; called King David to repentance; saved Daniel from the lions; parted the Red Sea; protected Shadrach, Meshach, and Abednego in Nebuchadnezzar's furnace; and raised Jesus from the dead. When any kind of ritual keeps us from expecting God's power in our midst, it has failed in its purpose.

The second reason Jesus gives for praying simply is that God already knows what we need—so the pressure of elaborate rituals to catch God's attention is gone. In most religions of Jesus' day, the gods wanted something from their worshipers and would not bestow favors freely.

The story of Gilgamesh comes to us from the time of the Babylonian empire, dating to approximately 1500 B.C., although it may be based on a much older tale from the Sumerian civilization dating to approximately 3000 B.C.[1] The story is similar to the biblical telling of Noah. In the *Epic of Gilgamesh*, however, Utnapishtim, the "Noah" of the story, is warned about the coming flood not because he is a good man, but because the gods know that if they destroy every human being there will be no one to offer sacrifices and the gods will starve and die. In this epic poem, as in many myths and legends, the gods required sacrifice and worship in order to live.[2]

In some ways, this is a comforting view. If my god needs something from me, then I can do something to earn his or her favor. Even today, some people believe that if they behave a certain way—if they tithe, live helpful lives, or don't do certain immoral things—God will look favorably on them. The truth of the matter is that we can do nothing to make God love us more or less. God loves us because God chooses to, and more, our heavenly Parent understands us and already knows what we need. There is no need to ramble on or dress our requests in fancy words. God wants us to pray simply and honestly, whether we offer praise, thanksgiving, or make a request.

Expanded translation
> When you pray, don't think you need to build up a whole ritual and mysterious way to contact God like the foreigners do, for they believe their gods will only answer if they make lots of noise. Don't make yourself like them, for your [pl.] Parent, who understands you better than you understand yourself, knows what you [sing.] need before you begin your prayers.

οὕτως οὖν προσεύχεσθε ὑμεῖς πάτερ ἡμῶν
ὁ ἐν τοῖς οὐρανοῖς ἁγιασθήτω τὸ ὄνομά σου
ἐλθέτω ἡ βασιλεία
σου γενηθήτω τὸ θέλημά σου
ὡς ἐν οὐρανῷ καὶ ἐπὶ γῆς
τὸν ἄρτον ἡμῶν τὸν ἐπιούσιον δὸς ἡμῖν σήμερον
καὶ ἄφες ἡμῖν τὰ ὀφειλήματα ἡμῶν
ὡς καὶ ἡμεῖς ἀφήκαμεν τοῖς ὀφειλέταις ἡμῶν
καὶ μὴ εἰσενέγκῃς ἡμᾶς εἰς πειρασμόν
ἀλλὰ ῥῦσαι ἡμᾶς ἀπὸ τοῦ πονηροῦ

Thus then you pray "Our Father
in heaven reverenced be your name.
Let come your kingdom
let come into being your will
as in heaven also on earth.
Our necessary bread give to us today;
and forgive us our debts
as also we forgive those owing us;
and do not bring us into temptation
but preserve us from [the] evil [one]."

Matthew 6:9-13 · The Lord's Prayer

Verse 9—Reverence for God

Verse 9 begins with *outós*, a word most simply translated "thus" but having other meanings as well. My favorite is "without further ado." Jesus begins his example prayer, "Without further ado, you (as opposed to the foreigners just mentioned) pray like this."

It is ironic that a prayer Jesus gives as a pattern of simplicity has become a ritualistic prayer, repeated in Christian circles for centuries. The Lord's Prayer does not appear to ever have been intended as ritual.

As to the prayer itself, most English translations have been heavily influenced by the Latin Vulgate, which begins: *Pater noster* (our Father) *qui in caelis es* (who is in heaven) *sanctificetur nomen tuum* (holy be your name). The Greek construction, however, is less elaborate. If we met it anywhere else, we would translate it simply as "our heavenly Parent."

The phrase "holy be your name" would have been a much more familiar construction to the first century hearers of this prayer. To invoke someone's name was to invoke the person. For instance, I can say, "Hello, my name is Karen," which tells you very little about me. However, if I say, "Hello, I'm Karen. I live in Oregon, in a cute little mobile home. I'm single and a librarian by profession; I think chocolate is one of the four major food groups; and my passion is writing," you know a lot more about me. The word *name* encompasses all that and more. Remember that the Jews won't even pronounce God's name, using only the letters YHWH to show their respect and reverence. If I am sent somewhere in someone's name, it means I have that person's authority to order what needs to be done. At the end of his written record, Matthew includes Jesus' commission to the remaining 11 disciples. Jesus sends them—and us—out to finish his work in his name and in the name of the other members of the Trinity. Reverencing God's name is not a simple or light prayer.

> Without further ado, pray like this: Our heavenly Parent, may you be reverenced because of who you are.

Verse 10—God's Kingdom and Will

Translating from the Greek, the next verse begins, "let your kingdom come into being." Is Jesus talking about the earthly kingdom of the millennium, the kingdom in our heart, the part of the kingdom he planned to usher in with his death and resurrection, or the kingdom that will come at the end of time? Since the rest of the sermon refers to what we do here on earth now, I suspect Jesus is mainly referring to the part of the kingdom that is us, his followers. Therefore, we pray that God's kingdom will grow on earth. We have an important role in answering this prayer, since God's kingdom grows as we live kingdom lives and invite others to join us.

Next, we pray that God's will be carried out. The picture here is of God as King with eager subjects waiting to know their sovereign's wishes so they can rush to carry them out. This is not a natural picture for those of us who grew up in a democracy. Perhaps a more natural image for us is of a loving child who does everything possible to please his or her parents, or doting parents who rush to appease every whim of their child. Alternatively, we might think of someone in love who delights in doing things to make his or her beloved happy, or a new parent who does everything possible to keep his or her newborn content. Here, too, we play a part.

The final phrase translates to "as in heaven, so on earth." The word for "heaven" is singular here. In Greek, when the Bible refers to what we call heaven, it is usually the plural: "our Parent, the one in the heavens." When used in the singular, especially when *earth* is in the sentence, it usually means "the whole of the created universe," that is, all of creation outside the earth. To Jesus' listeners *heaven* would have meant what they could see in the sky. Today, we know it refers to something on a scale they could not possibly imagine. The entire created universe does God's will automatically, so we pray that we will, too.

> May your kingdom come into being through us, as citizens of the kingdom. May your will be carried out by human beings as it is all over the created universe.

Verse 11—Our Daily Needs

The word we translate "bread," *artos*, can mean simply bread. It can also mean any kind of food, or a means of support and livelihood, similar to the way we say we "bring home the bacon."

Bread is a powerful symbol in the Bible. Think of the manna of the Old Testament that kept God's people alive during their travels. Jesus called himself the bread of life (John 6:35), and during the last Passover meal he ate with his disciples, he broke bread as the symbol of his body about to be broken. Bread is food for both body and soul.

The word we translate "daily" is used only in the Gospels; therefore, its meaning is determined by the text around it. It combines a preposition, meaning "near" or "toward," and a root word, meaning "that which has substance." Because this verse appears to point back to the manna, a better translation is "for our need." We ask God to sustain us today. We do not look to the future, but instead, like the Jews of old, we trust that we will be given what we need.

When I think of how much of my life is spent looking to the future—putting money away for retirement—as well as how much of my money is spent on "wants," this verse challenges me. Is it morally sound to have thousands of dollars tied up to ensure my future when my brothers and sisters live in poverty? Or am I just being prudent? Is it morally sound to remodel my house, buy a better car or more clothes that I don't really need? What does it really mean to trust God to provide my daily needs? These are difficult questions we should all consider as we pray this prayer of promise.

Give us what we need for today, both physically and spiritually.

Verse 12—Forgiveness

> There's no point in burying the hatchet if you're going to put up a marker on the site. (Sydney Harris)

What does it mean to forgive a debt? If I borrow $5.00 from someone and she tells me, "Just forget it; you don't have to pay me back," she has forgiven my debt. To forgive is to release from obligation or consequence, to cancel, or to remit. Once we forgive someone, it's over and done—that person is free from obligation to us. When we grit our teeth and say, "I forgive you," but never forget the injury, we haven't really forgiven.

Sometimes the injury done to us is so deep it takes forgiving people more than once. In experiences where I was treated quite poorly, more than once I thought I had forgiven the offender. Still, every time I thought about him or her, I got angry. It wasn't until I was finally able to get past the final barrier and truly forgive that the anger, hurt, and feelings of victimization disappeared and I felt freedom.

Sometimes we enjoy being a victim. It can make us feel noble, and forgiving someone means letting that go. Sometimes we feel that forgiving someone makes us look weak. Indeed, forgiveness can take courage. But without forgiveness there is no reconciliation.

We are to forgive debts and obligations. The sermon's parallel passage, Luke 11:4, substitutes the Greek word for "sin," a moral lapse rather than a deliberate act. In the eyes of heaven, when someone does something to hurt us he or she now owes us debt. We can cancel that debt if we will. Wouldn't it be a beautiful world where forgiveness and reconciliation were the rule? We can do our part to bring that vision to reality.

> Don't hold us accountable for our moral lapses, even as we also don't hold others accountable when they don't treat us as they should.

Verse 13—Protect Us

> I can resist everything except temptation. (Oscar Wilde)

We all know the power of temptation. Sometimes temptations are big, like grand theft, and sometimes small, like taking a couple extra mintues for our break. Temptations come in all shapes and sizes, from overindulgence in food to cheating on our taxes, from pornography to blaming someone else for our mistakes. We may be tempted to lie to the boss—or for the boss. We may be tempted to take the easy way, to do what we know is wrong in order to fit in, to lie to escape blame, or to skate on morally thin ice when it helps us gain power. James 1:14-15 explains how we are tempted: "But each one is tempted when, by his own evil desire, he is dragged away and enticed. Then, after desire has conceived, it gives birth to sin; and sin, when it is full-grown, gives birth to death."

Though we can be tempted by almost anything, most of us face particular temptations based on our personalities. Like lures to fish or bait in a trap, these temptations promise something good but instead deliver pain and death. Just as a fish is safer nowhere near the hook, so we pray to not be led into the presence of that which tempts us.

Notice that we don't pray for the temptation to be removed. Often, a temptation is the result of something good or of something natural used wrongly. When we need comfort, we may turn to food instead of friends. The gift of discernment, or the ability to see to the heart of something, can be misused so that we become critical and judgmental.

What we pray for then is threefold. We pray to not be put into a place where we are tempted to do wrong, and we pray to not be tempted to use our natural needs and gifts wrongly. We also ask to be preserved from the evil one. "Evil one" is one of the names for Satan in the Bible; it can also include a person tempting us to do wrong, or the temptation to do wrong that springs up in our own hearts and minds.

Jesus says we must take temptation seriously enough to pray that we not be led into its presence.

> Don't bring us into a place where we are tempted to do wrong,
> but protect us from the one intending evil.

Expanded translation

> Without further ado, pray like this:
>
> Our heavenly Parent, may you be reverenced because of who you are.
>
> May your kingdom come into being through us, as citizens of the kingdom.

May your will be carried out by human beings as it is all over the created universe.

Give us what we need for today, both physically and spiritually.

Don't hold us accountable for our moral lapses, even as we also don't hold others accountable when they don't treat us as they should.

Don't bring us into a place where we are tempted to do wrong, but protect us from the one intending evil.

The Authorized or King James Version adds, "For thine is the kingdom, and the power, and the glory, for ever. Amen." This version of the Bible was translated in the 1600s when only a single Greek manuscript of the Bible existed, the Tischendorf manuscript. Other, older manuscripts that do not contain this phrase have since been found. Scholars believe this phrase was not originally part of the Lord's Prayer, and was likely added when these verses were used in the corporate prayer life of the early church.[3]

ἐὰν γὰρ ἀφῆτε τοῖς ἀνθρώποις
τὰ παραπτώματα αὐτῶν ἀφήσει καὶ ὑμῖν
ὁ πατὴρ ὑμῶν ὁ οὐράνιος
ἐὰν δὲ μὴ ἀφῆτε τοῖς ἀνθρώποις οὐδὲ
ὁ πατὴρ ὑμῶν ἀφήσει τὰ παραπτώματα ὑμῶν

For if you forgive the people
their wronging forgive also you
your heavenly Father
but if you do not forgive the people, neither
[will] your Father forgive your wrongdoing.

Matthew 6:14-15 · More Words on Forgiveness

Many promising reconciliations have broken down because while both parties come prepared to forgive, neither party come prepared to be forgiven. (Charles Williams)

What a remarkable set of verses these are! God allows us to set the terms for forgiveness. We don't have to beg or plead or perform remarkable deeds. We must only be willing to forgive those who hurt us.

In Matthew 18:21-35, Jesus tells the parable of a servant who owed his master a huge debt impossible for him to pay. The servant begged for more time and so the master took pity on him and canceled the debt completely. The servant then left his master and ran into a fellow servant who owed him a few dollars. When the man couldn't pay immediately, the servant had him thrown into debtor's prison. The master got wind of the action and was understandably angry. He had the unmerciful servant thrown into debtor's prison himself until he could pay back every cent. This is the first viewpoint: We owe God so much for forgiving us that any forgiveness we owe others is very small by comparison. We are to show the family characteristic of forgiveness to any who need it from us, or we may find our own forgiveness rescinded.

This is not a threat (forgive or you won't be forgiven), but merely a statement of how forgiveness works. There are serious offenses—often one-sided—that need forgiveness, such as rape, betrayal, murder. At the same time, forgiving someone releases us from the victim role and allows us to see things more clearly—including what we may have done to contribute to the problem. It may very well be that the other person sees me as the aggressor, and I may need to ask for his or her forgiveness too. In the end, it is all about restoring relationship.

In C.S. Lewis's *The Great Divorce*, those in hell visit heaven for a short time and may stay in heaven under certain conditions. One man had been a boss on earth. He arrives in heaven and is met by one of his former employees, who at one time had hated him. Len, the former employee, has been forgiven for his hatred and is marvelously happy. But the former boss can neither give nor accept forgiveness. He's too busy looking for his "rights," and in the end chooses to go back to hell rather than accept the joys of heaven.[4] Demanding our rights and insisting we are completely right and others completely wrong leaves us miserably locked into the victim role and traps us in unhappiness.

Not only can accepting forgiveness free us, forgiving others frees us too. The hurt and the debt between people is like a rope tying them together. By cutting this rope via forgiveness, both people are freed—the victim *and* the aggressor. If we value our freedom from emotional baggage, then forgiveness is also in our own best interest.

There are times when forgiveness must be followed by tough action, such as when the forgiveness involves those for whom using others is a way of life. If you are forgiving someone over and over for the same offense, it may be time to take other action—perhaps walking away and insisting he or she finds help. Forgiveness should be a way of taking responsibility, not of evading it; a way to freedom, not a cage.

A woman owed a contractor a large sum for work he had done on her house. He tried to get the money from her but she kept giving him one excuse after another. His anger with her began affecting his attitude toward the world until he finally made the decision that the work he had done for her was a gift. He literally forgave her the debt she owed him and found himself free of anger and frustration. Years later, she was convicted about what she had done to this contractor and came to him in tears to ask forgiveness and pay him. "You were forgiven long ago," he told her serenely, "and the work I did for you is my gift to you."

Forgiveness is a golden key that will unlock a prison door, a knife that will cut a binding cord, one of the most powerful tools we have to restore relationships, and a very good way to model the behavior of our heavenly Parent.

Expanded translation

> If you don't keep accounts concerning those who have hurt you, your heavenly Parent will also wipe the slate clean for you. Until you wipe the slate clean concerning what others have done to you, you won't be able to see your own failures and turn to your heavenly Parent for pardon.

13

TEACHING ON FASTING

ὅταν δὲ νηστεύητε μὴ γίνεσθε ὡς οἱ ὑποκριταὶ σκυθρωποί
ἀφανίζουσιν γὰρ τὰ πρόσωπα αὐτῶν ὅπως φανῶσιν τοῖς ἀνθρώποις νηστεύοντες
ἀμὴν λέγω ὑμῖν ἀπέχουσιν τὸν μισθὸν αὐτῶν
σὺ δὲ νηστεύων ἄλειψαί σου τὴν κεφαλὴν καὶ τὸ πρόσωπόν σου νίψαι ὅπως μὴ φανῇς τοῖς ἀνθρώποις νηστεύων ἀλλὰ τῷ πατρί σου τῷ ἐν τῷ κρυφαίῳ καὶ ὁ πατήρ σου ὁ βλέπων ἐν τῷ κρυφαίῳ ἀποδώσει σοι

But when you fast, do not become as the playactors
gloomy and sullen
for they disfigure their faces for the purpose of
being seen by people fasting.
Truly I say to you they have their reward.
But you fasting, anoint your head
and your face wash so that you are not revealed

> to people fasting, and your Father
> seeing in secret will reward you.

Matthew 6:16-18 · High Tragedy

The third and last of Jesus' admonitions against performing acts of piety in public has to do with fasting. These verses are a little more difficult since few of us in the Christian church today practice fasting regularly.

These verses are again directed toward those who want to be admired for their piety. When these people fast they look anemic and deprived, obviously suffering for the sake of their religion. Since pious Jews fasted twice a week, on Tuesdays and Fridays, these playactors got a lot of practice!

The word translated "disfigured" or "sad" may refer to the masks in ancient Greek drama. In effect, these people don the tragedy mask to indicate to everyone the part they are playing that day. Jesus says that when we do this—just as when we pray on street corners and use many elaborate words—we have had our reward and our accounts are marked "paid in full." Instead, we are to fast as a secret spiritual discipline before God only and leave the reward up to our heavenly Parent.

Jesus never commands fasting as he commands other things, such as forgiveness. We know he did fast; likely, he participated in the usual fasts before he began his ministry. Then after his baptism by John, he went into the wilderness for a 40-day fast, preparing himself for the task ahead and perhaps defining it. This is described in the first 11 verses of Matthew chapter 4.

What is the importance of the discipline of fasting? Let me suggest several purposes.

First, fasting breaks our routine, forcing us to refocus. This is always good for us, particularly if we spend the time we normally spend eating to focus on God. We may ordinarily grab a snack at work, eat while working, eat supper while watching television, or eat fast food for lunch every day. How could we take that same time and instead focus on God, friends, family, or other relationships?

Another purpose for fasting is to show us what we value and to what we give most of our energy. This may be work, television, food, shopping, gossip, or checking out the latest celebrity or the latest court trial. Choosing something we do frequently and stopping that activity as a spiritual discipline can help us focus on how we should live our lives as kingdom citizens.

Fasting can help build discipline into our life. Athletes know the value of discipline. Musicians know the value of discipline. Any career that requires years of preparation and practice teaches the value of discipline. Fasting is another way we bring discipline to our life and our Christian walk.

Fasting is also a countercultural activity that helps free us from dependence on the world's values. As is taught all throughout the sermon, citizens of the kingdom are to live differently from the world. We must live according to different values and rules.

Today, we may fast regularly; some practice this spiritual discipline. We may also choose to fast in particular circumstances such as when we need to make a big decision or when our heart is weighed down with important considerations. Sometimes we choose to go without a meal to donate money to the poor and needy.

There are many types of fasting, such as refraining from something to strengthen our relationship with God or refraining from one thing to do something more important.

As I write this, I am doing an unplanned and unanticipated fast from my normal activity. I broke my arm a week ago, and have had to rest a few days. Today is the first day I have been able to type at any length. Through this time of fasting, God is teaching me many things:

- I am no longer twenty and will have to slow down as I walk up or down the stairs where I tripped.
- Pride is a worthless commodity when I need help from others to do things I would like to do for myself.

- I must learn to do without some things and to do other things more slowly.
- I must be patient as I wait for my arm to heal completely.
- My friends and church family are a wonderful, true blessing when I am so far away from my biological family.

As another transition verse, Matthew 6:16-18, points back to Jesus' words on giving and praying simply and privately, and points toward his teaching on learning to trust God to take care of us.

Expanded translation

And whenever you fast, do not look excessively depressed as the playactors do; for they love to don the tragedy mask (hiding their true self), playing to the admiring crowd. Truly, I tell you, their account has been marked "paid in full." But whenever you fast, get ready for the day just like normal, washing your face and combing your hair, so nobody has a clue you are fasting except your hidden heavenly Parent. And your Parent, who likewise works behind the scenes, will see to your reward.

14

TEACHING ON THINGS

μὴ θησαυρίζετε ὑμῖν θησαυροὺς
ἐπὶ τῆς γῆς ὅπου σὴς καὶ
βρῶσις ἀφανίζει
καὶ ὅπου κλέπται διορύσσουσιν καὶ κλέπτουσιν
θησαυρίζετε δὲ ὑμῖν θησαυροὺς ἐν οὐρανῷ
ὅπου οὔτε σὴς οὔτε βρῶσις
ἀφανίζει
καὶ ὅπου κλέπται οὐ διορύσσουσιν
οὐδὲ κλέπτουσιν ὅπου
γάρ ἐστιν ὁ θησαυρός σου
ἐκεῖ ἔσται καὶ ἡ καρδία σου

Do not store up for yourself treasure
upon the earth where moths and
their eating can [make garments] disappear
and where thieves break in and steal.
But store up for yourself treasure in heaven
where moths and their eating do not
[make garments] disappear
and where thieves do not break in

> nor steal for where your treasure is
> There is also your heart.

Matthew 6:19-21 · Where is Our Treasure?

> This world is not my home, I'm just a-passing through.
> My treasures are laid up somewhere beyond the blue.
> The angels beckon me from heaven's open door,
> And I can't feel at home in this world anymore.
>
> (J.R. Baxter, Jr., "This World is Not My Home")

Matthew 6:19-21 makes me curious. The people to whom Jesus is talking would have been poor enough by the world's standards. If he felt it important to warn these poverty-stricken people about materialism, what implications might his words have for us today?

This section reminds me of the parable in Luke 12:13-21 about a farmer who had a prosperous year. He built bigger barns to hold his bumper crop and then settled back, ready to enjoy life. But God called him a fool, for bigger barns on earth would mean nothing when he died.

When I was a child, my family had a cottage near a pine forest. I would heap up pine needles into the outline of a house and play there happily, or I would drape a sheet over a clothesline to make a tent. I could line up chairs and be a bus driver or line up my dolls and be a teacher in a classroom. I sometimes think God looks at our efforts to surround ourselves with perishable comforts in the same way, as just playing pretend.

Deep in our hearts we know there is no security on this earth. Everything is subject to the "moth," that is, natural forces such as earthquakes, volcanoes, storms, disease, or just plain decay. We also face "thieves"—robbers, wars, or terrorist attacks. Believing that anything on earth can give us real security is just so much pretending. As citizens of the kingdom, we know our real lives lie elsewhere.

When we read the Bible, we discover that it doesn't teach thrift or hoarding, but rather generosity. From the Jubilee law that mandated all lands be periodically returned to their original owners, to the rules of gleaning that said a farmer was to leave the parts of his crop on the edges for the poor, to Jesus' approval of the woman who poured expensive perfume on his feet, we must learn to hold material possessions lightly.

In the last chapter we talked about fasting. Going without food may be difficult, but going without money is even more frightening. Money carries so many meanings—security, prestige, power, and independence. But Jesus views money and the things money can buy as mere possessions that wear out and have to be protected from thieves. The person who dies with the most toys does *not* win in the economy of God.

How do we provide for ourselves treasures in heaven? The teaching of Matthew 6 suggests that one way is through the secret good we do for others—the good only our heavenly Parent sees. We find a similar suggestion in James 2:15-16: "Suppose a brother or sister is without clothes and daily food. If one of you says to him, 'Go, I wish you well; keep warm and well fed,' but does nothing about his physical needs, what good is it?" When we see a need and meet it, we lay up treasure in heaven. When we work to establish God's kingdom by reaching out to others, whether they need physical help or just someone to listen, we lay up treasure in heaven. We lay up treasure in heaven by tithing and serving in our local church. We lay up treasure in heaven when we share the good news of God's love with others. Through holding our possessions lightly, we can also build up treasures in heaven by giving to those in need. In his book *The Scandal of the Evangelical Conscience*, Ron Sider writes that if all Americans who call themselves Christians simply tithed, there would be 143 billion dollars available to help the poor and disenfranchised.[1] This is a scandal indeed, that so many go unhelped because of our lack of generosity.

Quaker tradition uses queries to think through values. These are especially relevant to where our treasures lie:

- Do you have poor in your church? Have you sought to find that out?

- Do you have poor in the neighborhood of your church or your home? In your city or town?
- Do you go where you can see and be touched by the poverty of others?
- Do your spending habits reflect the world's values or the values of God's kingdom?
- Have you become numb to the needs around you?
- Do you model a caring attitude before your children?

Using these queries to consider our own values, we must continue to strive after seeing the world as true kingdom citizens.

Expanded translation

> Your most precious possession, whether that's clothing, money, stocks, or security, should not be anything able to be stored up on earth where it is vulnerable to decay, acts of nature, and theft. Rather, your most precious possessions should be stored up in heaven where they are not vulnerable to decay, acts of nature, and theft. What's most precious to you is what you are going to be thinking about and working for most often, so make sure it is something worth thinking about and working for—full of kingdom values.

ὁ λύχνος τοῦ σώματός ἐστιν ὁ ὀφθαλμός
ἐὰν οὖν ᾖ ὁ ὀφθαλμός σου ἁπλοῦς
ὅλον τὸ σῶμά σου φωτεινὸν ἔσται
ἐὰν δὲ ὁ ὀφθαλμός σου πονηρὸς ᾖ
ὅλον τὸ σῶμά σου σκοτεινὸν ἔσται
εἰ οὖν τὸ φῶς τὸ ἐν σοὶ
σκότος ἐστίν τὸ σκότος πόσον

The light of the body is the eye.
If therefore is your eye single,
all your body is illuminated.
But if your eye is unhealthy
all your body is darkened.
If therefore the light in you
darkness is how great a darkness [it is].

Matthew 6:22-23 · Keep Your Glass Clean

We believe as Christians that Jesus has given us the ideal eyes by which to see the real nature of reality. (Richard Rohr)

From treasure, Jesus turns to the human body. Sight is one of the main ways we interact with the world, so as long as our eyes are "single"—that is, serving their intended purpose—they allow us to see, just as oil lamps lit up the insides of the houses of Jesus' listeners.

There are several ways to think about an eye being single. First, most literally, we can control what we see. We can refrain from looking at pornography and stay away from X-rated movies and other images that detract from our ability to be whole-hearted Christ followers. The Bible tells us in Philippians 4:8: "Finally, brothers, whatever is true, whatever is noble, whatever is right, whatever is pure, whatever is lovely, whatever is admirable—if anything is excellent or praiseworthy—think about such things."

Second, we can try to see those we meet as fellow children of God. We can look past imperfections and irritating mannerisms, and remember that God loves them. Seeing the world as God sees it should be our goal as followers of Christ.

We must also not shut our eyes to the needs around us. It is easy to let ourselves become so absorbed in our own problems that we don't notice those who need our help. We sometimes allow ourselves to be isolated in our own little worlds and in our own routines, not seeing needs because we never go where the needs are.

It is also easy to run the danger of seeing people as stereotypes instead of individuals. Because of these stereotypes we may even allow ourselves to become afraid of people—gays, blacks, Muslims or other religious groups, those who enter our country without proper papers, liberals, and conservatives, or any group that we have been taught to see as inferior to ourselves in a moral or religious sense. God does not see us as stereotypes, and neither should we look at each other so. This is one reason many Quakers take a stand against war—soldiers are taught to see the enemy as evil and inferior, therefore justifying hate and killing.

Matthew 6:22-23 ends with the warning that if our eyes are diseased, our body will be gloomy. This is the real danger: that we see the world wrongly without knowing it. If we realize we are in darkness we can open the shades or turn on the light. But if we believe we are already in the light, we will simply go on the way we are. Like Plato's analogy of people trapped in a cave who believe the shadows on the wall are reality and so don't believe in a real world of light, we can stop recognizing truth.

In *The Silver Chair*, one of C.S. Lewis' Narnia books, Aslan sends two children to find a missing Narnian prince. With them goes Puddleglum, a gloomy but ultimately courageous fellow. In their search, the three end up deep underground as prisoners of the same witch who holds the prince captive. She tries to enchant them, throwing a magic powder on the fire to dull their senses while telling them that they have only imagined the world above. She maintains they have imagined a sun by seeing a lamp and they have imagined the great lion Aslan by seeing a cat. The three nearly succumb to this lie until Puddleglum stamps on the fire, waking them up. He declares, "I'm going to live like a Narnian as I can, even if there isn't any Narnia."[2] He decides to live a kingdom lifestyle, even in a world where God seems very far away. This is seeing with our spiritual eyes, seeing clearly, and seeing what is real by faith.

As we develop a single eye to see the world as God sees it, we understand more about being kingdom citizens. We grow in our own faith, and we become moved to reach out to those of our brothers and sisters who are still living in darkness.

Expanded translation

> You see everything through your eyes—they are like a lamp. If you are looking at the world as God looks at it, you are seeing properly, just like a properly trimmed wick creates a lamp that can light up the room. But if your eye is not working properly, that is, if you are not looking at the world as God does, all your body will be gloomy, because God is light. If you have accepted that gloom inside you as light you're in trouble because it won't occur to you to seek real light. You have doomed yourself to live in the half-light of half a life.

οὐδεὶς δύναται δυσὶ κυρίοις δουλεύειν
ἢ γὰρ τὸν ἕνα μισήσει
καὶ τὸν ἕτερον ἀγαπήσει
ἢ ἑνὸς ἀνθέξεται
καὶ τοῦ ἑτέρου καταφρονήσει
οὐ δύνασθε θεῷ δουλεύειν καὶ μαμωνᾷ

No one is able two masters to serve.
For either the one he will dislike
and the other he will love
or the one he will be devoted to
and the other he will despise.
You cannot serve God and mammon.

Matthew 6:24 · One Boss

Here, Jesus is talking about where our allegiance and our securities lie. The word most often translated as "money" is *mamonas*, sometimes spelled with a capital letter and two *m*s in the middle as *Mammonas*. Originally, this was the name of the Syrian god of riches. By Jesus' time the word was used like an eponym and meant food, maintenance, or provisions—that is, what is needed for physical life. We can look to created things for our security or we can look to the creator, but we cannot have it both ways.

This is a hard concept for those who hear self-indulgence exalted everywhere. We are often told to have things our way. We read books or go to seminars on success principles that teach us to tap into our own potential to do whatever we want to do. We buy into the world's definition of success, which involves a certain standard of living. We make sure our children are enrolled in the right schools and the right sports and we learn how to invest wisely—we absorb the standards of the world to a greater or lesser extent.

Jesus clearly teaches that citizens of the kingdom should have a different definition of success. If we think back to previous verses, we see clearly the criteria for a kingdom lifestyle: one that serves God, not the world. Blessed are the humble. Blessed are the merciful. Blessed are the peacemakers. Further on, we read Jesus' commands to love our enemies and to be generous. We reach out to others out of love instead of for the praise of others.

Jesus makes his point clear: We cannot hold dual citizenship. We are either citizens of the kingdom or citizens of the world. The aims of the two are diametrically opposed. Their views on success are opposite. Their rewards are completely different—the praise of people or God's approval.

There is a story from the time of the building of the cathedral of Milan. A journalist from Rome asked a stonecutter what he was doing. He replied, "I am crushing rock." The journalist asked a second man the same question. "I am working hard to make a good life for myself and my family." A third worker answered, "I am building a cathedral." While two of the workers saw only their mundane, everyday life, the third had the bigger picture in mind. No matter where we are or what we are doing, we should be able to say, "I am building God's kingdom," or "I am following where my master leads."

A friend of mine was filling out an information sheet prior to attending a college reunion. Under "occupation:" he wrote "Christ follower." What amazing things we could accomplish for God if we all felt that way.

Following Christ and living as a citizen of the kingdom is not a veneer of respectability and goodness laid over a worldly life. It is an entirely new attitude and new motivation. It is not just the difference between Donald Trump and Mother Teresa, but it involves living our lives with our focus on God. Kingdom citizens see families and friends and jobs and all parts of life as God sees them. We are not here to be successful according to the world's standards, but to be Jesus' hands and feet, ears, eyes, and mouth in a troubled world.

Matthew 6:24 serves as a transition between the metaphors of singleness of purpose and the final point of this chapter: depending on God to meet our needs. In this insecure world where we never really know from one minute to the next what is going to happen, it is comforting to know that we have someone in whom we can place complete trust. Material possessions can rust or be stolen, jobs come and go, our bodies betray us, those we love die or leave, but God is always here. If our trust is in God, we will better weather the storms that come our way.

Expanded translation

> No one can do a good job working for two bosses. For either he will like one a lot better than the other (and so work harder and better for that one); or be devoted to the one, caring very much about him or her, and have contempt for the other, hardly caring to be in the same room with him or her. You cannot hold dual citizenship in the world and the kingdom of God—your trust will be in one or the other; it can't be in both.

15

αβγδεζηθικλμνξοπρσστυφχψωαβγδεζηθικλμνξοπρσστυφχψωαβγδεζηθικλμνξοπρσστυφχψω

TEACHING ON TRUST

διὰ τοῦτο λέγω ὑμῖν
μὴ μεριμνᾶτε τῇ ψυχῇ ὑμῶν
τί φάγητε ἢ τί πίητε μηδὲ τῷ σώματι ὑμῶν
τί ἐνδύσησθε
οὐχὶ ἡ ψυχὴ πλεῖόν ἐστιν τῆς τροφῆς καὶ
τὸ σῶμα τοῦ ἐνδύματος
ἐμβλέψατε εἰς τὰ πετεινὰ τοῦ οὐρανοῦ
ὅτι οὐ σπείρουσιν
οὐδὲ θερίζουσιν οὐδὲ συνάγουσιν εἰς ἀποθήκας
καὶ ὁ πατὴρ ὑμῶν ὁ οὐράνιος τρέφει αὐτά
οὐχ ὑμεῖς μᾶλλον διαφέρετε αὐτῶν
τίς δὲ ἐξ ὑμῶν μεριμνῶν δύναται
προσθεῖναι ἐπὶ τὴν ἡλικίαν αὐτοῦ πῆχυν ἕνα

Because of this I am telling you
do not be anxious about your life
what you shall eat nor for your body
what you shall wear.
[Is] not your life more than food and

> the body [more] than clothing?
> Look at the birds of the sky.
> They do not plant seed;
> they neither reap nor gather into storehouses
> and your heavenly Father feeds them.
> Are you not more worth than them?
> But which of you being anxious is able
> to add to his lifespan one hour?

Matthew 6:25-27 · Consider the Wild Birds

**Worry does not empty tomorrow of its sorrow.
It empties today of its strength. (Corrie Ten Boom)**

Matthew 6:25 begins with *therefore* and ties in directly to the previous verses. Since our treasures are in heaven, since we are filled with the light of God's love and presence, and since we have determined to serve God, we don't have to worry about having our needs met.

The word translated "worry" or "anxious" is a little stronger in Greek. It means "be unduly concerned." It's all right to think about the future and make plans, but there is no need to panic, because we have the assurance that God will take care of us. Jesus says this to people in an occupied country where life is uncertain and control belongs only to the Roman overlords. If people were not to feel unduly anxious in this situation, then we can rest assured God will watch over us as well.

"Don't be unduly concerned about food and clothing," is the word from Jesus. Abraham Maslow was an early psychologist. He is most well known for his Hierarchy of Needs,[1] in which he postulated that, above all, people must have food, drink, and shelter before they can begin to grow and develop any further. God understands our need for basics, and gives us the guarantee of those needs being met when we follow the kingdom way.

Jesus makes several points. First is the comforting fact that God watches out for us, just as God does for the birds and the beasts. Since Jesus did most of his teaching outdoors, he could point to the wild birds flying overhead. The listeners could watch the birds as they thought about the fact that birds and beasts do not have to toil to grow crops. God provides food for them. How can we believe God cares less for us?

Second, there is more to life than what we eat or wear. As citizens of the kingdom, we don't have the same values as the world around us. We don't need to buy the latest fashions when our closet is already full of perfectly good clothing. We don't need fifty pairs of shoes. We don't need the latest gadget. All of us must learn for ourselves where the line falls between need and self-indulgence. This is especially true in American culture. Do we really need a house worth half a million dollars? Do we really need designer clothing? Do we really need to buy a new phone to get all the new features? Do we think about the millions in the world who live on less than a dollar a day when we find something we think we can't live without? We must remember that this world is not our final home and there may be better, more important things to do with our money than buying something we don't really need.

That brings us to Jesus' third point, more implied than stated. In this world today, we are Jesus' hands and feet to help others. God may ask us to meet the basic needs of someone else who has less than we do or is in a tight spot. If we all made it our business to see that everyone had his or her basic needs met, remarkable things could be accomplished, for God often provides for our needs through the faithfulness of the kingdom's other citizens.

With the last verse in this section, Jesus comes back to undue concern. Though the verse is a little odd—it actually says "add eighteen inches to his lifespan," which could mean either "add eighteen inches to his height" or "add a little time to his lifespan"—the basic meaning is clear enough. I can sit around and worry about whether I am going to make ends meet, but that doesn't get me any closer to meeting my needs. I can worry about tomorrow's exam, but all the worry does is rob me of needed sleep. I can worry about a child out after hours, but it doesn't bring him or her back any sooner. Sometimes we can harness our concern to get us moving to solve a problem, but worry itself fixes nothing.

Expanded translation

> Because [you have chosen the kingdom way], I am telling you, don't be unduly concerned about having enough to eat, or about what you are going to wear. You'll agree it takes more than just food to keep body and soul together, won't you, and that there's more to your body than what you're wearing? Look overhead—see the wild birds wheeling above us? They don't [have to] plant crops, or harvest the grain, or store it up for the winter and [yet] your heavenly Parent provides all that they need. Think of the difference between birds and people—you are worth infinitely more, more than you can possibly realize at this moment. Which of you [gathered here] by undue concern is able to add a single hour to his lifespan?

καὶ περὶ ἐνδύματος τί μεριμνᾶτε
καταμάθετε τὰ κρίνα τοῦ ἀγροῦ
πῶς αὐξάνουσιν οὐ κοπιῶσιν οὐδὲ νήθουσιν
λέγω δὲ ὑμῖν ὅτι οὐδὲ Σολομὼν
ἐν πάσῃ τῇ δόξῃ αὐτοῦ περιεβάλετο
ὡς ἓν τούτων
εἰ δὲ τὸν χόρτον τοῦ ἀγροῦ
σήμερον ὄντα καὶ αὔριον
εἰς κλίβανον βαλλόμενον
ὁ θεὸς οὕτως ἀμφιέννυσιν οὐ πολλῷ μᾶλλον
ὑμᾶς ὀλιγόπιστοι

And [why] about clothing are you so concerned?
Observe the wildflowers of the field
how they grow; they neither toil nor spin.
But I tell you that not Solomon
in all his splendor arrayed himself
as [beautifully as] one of those.
And if the grass of the field
[which] exists today and the next day
into the oven is thrown,
God thus clothes how much more
[will God clothe] you, you of little faith?

Matthew 6:28-30 · Consider the Wildflowers

The miracles of nature do not seem miracles because they are so common. If no one had ever seen a flower, even a dandelion would be the most startling event in the world. (Unknown)

From food, Jesus now turns to clothing. "Look around you at the wildflowers," he says. I love flowers. Of cultivated flowers, roses are my favorite, not so much for their looks as for their wonderful scent.

I grew up near Rochester, New York, where there is a huge lilac park. In late spring gorgeous blooms cover the hillsides; blossoms of palest pink to deepest purple, all releasing their heady fragrance into the air. In Brooks, Oregon, there is an iris test garden. Before visiting there, I assumed all irises were purple, but I found that they grow in an astonishing variety of colors. They are well-named after the Greek word for "rainbow." Many of the tulip and daffodil bulbs sold across the United States are grown in Marysville, Washington, where huge fields of single colors—all pink, all yellow, all red—bloom in early spring.

Yet, with all the splendors of these beautiful places, there is something special about wildflowers. Who, seeing fields covered in the bright red, yellow, blue, gold, and green of summer blossoms or the pale pastel glories of the Oregon coast in spring, could really mourn for cultivated flowers? With all our technological skills, we still can't create anything as beautiful and fragile as a foxglove, a blue cornflower, or a black-eyed Susan.

One of the characteristics that make flowers so special is their shortness of season. We can force them in a greenhouse, of course, but to see tulips or buttercups or roses or lilacs or cherry blossoms, we must be at the right place at the right time. One of the indications of God's love for us is that God made even the transitory flowers so beautiful. Indeed, some of God's most beautiful creations have the shortest lifespans. Butterflies, surely some of the most colorful animals, live only days in that form. Delicate cherry blossoms in the spring are also at their height for only days.

Jesus then mentions the grass. In wood-poor Palestine, grass was gathered, dried, and burnt for fuel. We may not see flowers on the tall grass, but it is graceful in its own way, gleaming in the sun or waving in the wind.

This verse also reminds us of the transitory nature of our own lives. In Job 14:1-2 we read, "Man born of woman is of few days and full of trouble. He springs up like a flower and withers away; like a fleeting shadow, he does not endure," When we consider the whole timeline of human history, our life expectancy is really a very short time. But our real home is in heaven, and there is nothing to complain about, nothing to fear.

Jesus says that God's care of the natural world should be evidence enough that God will take care of us. The end of verse 30 is translated, "How much more will he clothe you, you of little faith?" The Greek for the final phrase is actually a single word, "little-faiths." When I see things happening in the world and I become fearful because I can't control those things, when problems come up or a friend betrays me, I feel like a little-faith. But God has put examples of God's care all around us. God cares for us and is in control.

In earthquakes, tsunamis, floods, volcanoes, fires, and other natural disasters, God is in control. In the midst of plagues and illness, God is in control. When the stock market crashes, or bombs go off—whatever happens around us—we can rest assured that God has not forsaken us. We must live our lives moment by moment as time ticks on, so this can be hard to understand. Yet God *is*, and that's a great comfort to finite mortals, we who live and die in our small slice of history. Our lives may be as brief as the wildflowers', but we are loved.

Expanded translation

> And why are you unduly concerned about clothing? Look around you at the ground. Think about how the wildflowers grow. They don't [have to] wear themselves out working long, hard hours, nor do they spin [fibers into cloth]. And I am telling you, not even Solomon in all his magnificence clothed himself [as gloriously] as one of these [little wildflowers]. And if God clothes in this manner the grass of the field, which exists for such a short time before being used for fuel, how much more surely [will God clothe] you? Don't you understand, you who have so little trust in your heavenly Parent, that God will take care of you as well as God takes care of the birds and flowers?

μὴ οὖν μεριμνήσητε λέγοντες
τί φάγωμεν ἢ τί πίωμεν
ἢ τί περιβαλώμεθα
πάντα γὰρ ταῦτα τὰ ἔθνη ἐπιζητοῦσιν
οἶδεν γὰρ ὁ πατὴρ ὑμῶν ὁ οὐράνιος
ὅτι χρῄζετε τούτων ἁπάντων

Therefore, do not be unduly concerned, saying,
"What shall we eat?" or "What shall we drink?"
or "What shall we wear?"
For all these things people desire.
For knows your heavenly Father
that you need all of these things.

Matthew 6:31-32 · Stop Your Worrying!

I think these difficult times have helped me to understand better than before how infinitely rich and beautiful life is in every way and that so many things that one goes around worrying about are of no importance whatsoever. (Isak Dinesen)

Once again Jesus reminds us that we don't have to worry about our basic needs being met. In the Greek the word *worry* means, "be unduly concerned," so Jesus isn't telling us we should never think about food, drink, or clothing. It's just that thoughts about such things should not be at the center of life.

Jesus notes that everybody needs food, water and clothing. God is well aware of this. But for those outside the kingdom, the desire for things can become the most important motivation in their life. People want only the best food and are constantly looking for new taste sensations. We drink exotic beverages—from teas, wines and fruit juices, to soft drinks. Even water has to be bottled and come from a certain spring. People spend a fortune on designer clothing. We own gadgets now that no one dreamed of in Jesus' day: cell phones, computers, video games, and cars. It isn't that we should not have wholesome food and drink and clothes that fit, but perhaps we need to consider how much is enough.

For a couple years after I moved to my present house, I was poorer than I have ever been. I often questioned whether I could afford a $3.00 pair of slacks at Goodwill and kept the thermostat set at 50 degrees in the winter only because it couldn't be turned down any lower. I was forced to step outside the materialism of Western culture, and much will never be the same for me. I learned a lot about trust and the kindness of others. I became thankful for little things and realized how much I still have to be thankful for even in my poorest times. I learned how to give out of my poverty and give creatively without money—sharing baked goods or my computer skills. These experiences taught me the important truths in these verses.

God can be trusted. We can step away from our culture and live the countercultural lifestyle Jesus expounds upon in the sermon. We can start in small ways by reaching out to others, being thoughtful about our purchases, giving just a little bit more than we think we can afford, and asking ourselves what we need instead of what we want. If nothing else, we can learn to give thanks more liberally and to appreciate what we have. We are kingdom citizens. Let us live like it.

Expanded translation

> In view of what I've just been saying about the wild birds and wildflowers you should have figured out by now that you don't have to be unduly concerned about your needs being met. You shouldn't be asking such questions as, "Where shall we find enough to eat?" or "Where are we going to get something to drink?" or "What in the world are we going to wear?" Those outside God's family think only of eating and drinking and the latest fashions. [Don't you worry about that sort of thing], for your heavenly Parent [already] knows all your needs.

ζητεῖτε δὲ πρῶτον τὴν βασιλείαν καὶ
τὴν δικαιοσύνην αὐτοῦ καὶ
ταῦτα πάντα προστεθήσεται ὑμῖν
μὴ οὖν μεριμνήσητε
εἰς τὴν αὔριον ἡ γὰρ αὔριον
μεριμνήσει ἑαυτῆς
ἀρκετὸν τῇ ἡμέρᾳ ἡ κακία αὐτῆς

But seek first the kingdom and
his righteousness [or justice] and
all these things shall be added to you.
Therefore, do not be unduly concerned
about tomorrow, for tomorrow
will be concerned for itself.
Enough for the day is its [own] misfortune.

Matthew 6:33-34 · Seek the Kingdom

In chapter 5 of Matthew the theme verse was verse 48, where Jesus summed up the previous teaching by telling us to grow up and to become mature in our attitude toward others. In the same way, verse 33 is the theme verse for chapter 6.

The beginning of chapter 6 warned about not doing acts of piety for people's praise. We are to give, pray, and fast in secret, looking for God's approval alone. Then Jesus reminded us to store our treasures in heaven where they are safe, rather than on earth where they are subject to wear and theft. All of the above is summed up in the beginning of verse 33, "But seek the kingdom and his righteousness/justice." The last part of the verse, "and all these things shall be added to you," refers to the section about our everyday needs.

We are to concern ourselves with working toward the establishment of God's kingdom in its double aspect—the inward purity of heart and the outward justice for all—both of which are contained in the word *dikaiosuné* often translated "righteousness." We don't have to be unduly concerned about the normal, everyday needs of life because we serve a God who feeds the wild birds and dresses common wildflowers in a splendor greater than that of the most famous human celebrity. God's provisions would have been a familiar concept to Jesus' listeners because of the stories of their ancestors' 40 years of wandering in the wilderness after leaving Egypt. There the Israelites learned to rely on God to provide food for them in the form of manna, as recorded in the book of Exodus in the Old Testament. Since the manna would spoil if kept overnight, they had to trust God to provide each and every day. So must we.

When Jesus says, "Don't be unduly concerned," he is not making a gentle suggestion. The phase is a prohibition in Greek, or a negative command. "*Do not* be unduly concerned," Jesus commands us.

Anxiety or fear does not help us meet what is coming. Marva Dawn, in her book *Joy in Our Weakness*, puts it well: "The Spirit's words remind us that fear about what we might experience does not really help us endure the suffering. Rather our fear does the reverse—it makes the suffering more difficult to bear."[2] We are more ready to meet whatever life brings if we approach life calmly, trusting God.

Expanded translation

> But your first desire should be for God's kingdom to be established and God's idea of justice and righteousness to come about. Don't worry about basic needs—God will see that they are met. And don't waste your time worrying about what might happen tomorrow, for you can't really guess accurately what will take place in the future. You will find enough to handle dealing with what really occurs without borrowing trouble.

Matthew 7

In Matthew 6, Jesus concentrated mainly on our attitudes. He talked about the heart from which acts of piety come and how we are to trust God for our needs and seek to build the kingdom. By the end of the chapter, we have been taught to straighten our priorities and realize God will take care of us. Lest we begin to think this makes us somehow special, we will move next into a portion of the sermon warning us to not judge others.

In Matthew 7, Jesus discusses our actions involving others, culminating with what we now call the Golden Rule. He then reminds us that the kingdom lifestyle requires deliberate choices and that what we do is more important than what we say. The section ends with the metaphor of the builders.

16

A Reminder about
RELATING TO OTHERS

μὴ κρίνετε ἵνα μὴ κριθῆτε
ἐν ᾧ γὰρ κρίματι
κρίνετε κριθήσεσθε καὶ
ἐν ᾧ μέτρῳ μετρεῖτε
μετρηθήσεται ὑμῖν

Judge not in order that you not be judged.
For by what means of judgment
you judge, you shall be judged, and
by what means of measurement you measure
shall it be measured to you.

Matthew 7:1-2 · Avoiding Judgment

If there's one thing human beings are good at, it is judging others. Jesus discussed this in the fifth chapter of Matthew; now he repeats it to emphasize its importance. Here, he speaks specifically about both the Pharisees and those of us who think we are superior.

The Greek word for "judge," *krino*, is not automatically negative. Like our English word *criticism*, it can run the gamut from "thoughtful consideration," to "condemn." It seems clear, however, that here Jesus uses the negative connotations of the word. He gives us a good practical reason not to condemn others—because it opens us up to condemnation in turn. This is like the forgiveness part of the Lord's Prayer in 6:14-15: We are forgiven the same way we forgive others. We are judged with the same criteria we use to judge others.

Verse 2 is an example of parallelism, a poetic device common in Old Testament writings and in the Psalms, where an author says the same thing twice in different words with slightly different meanings. Jesus uses parallelism here when he talks about judging and measuring. Sometimes we actively judge people, but other times we sit back and silently measure them against internal criteria to see if they pass or fail in relation to us. But as with the principles of generosity, if we are judgmental and critical of others they are likely to be judgmental and critical of us. If, on the other hand, we treat others with kindness and respect, as Jesus did, we are much more likely to receive kindness and respect in return. Jesus is ultimately talking about God, who will judge us as we have judged others.

"To measure" can also mean "to prepare a certain amount of goods to give to someone." If we give little and grudgingly, we can expect to receive little in return. If we give generously of our time, our money, or other resources, we can expect to receive generously in our own time of need.

Chapter 7 of Matthew, along the rest of the sermon, addresses making important choices. We can choose to be critical and judgmental or we can choose to be accepting and loving. No one was required to clean up his or her act before approaching Jesus. Jesus accepted all kinds of people—the morally impure; the physically diseased; and those the society considered of less value, such as women and children. He spoke with and helped political enemies and held up a Roman officer as an example of faith. In one of his more well-known parables, a despised Samaritan became an example of neighborliness. So we should accept others as fellow children of God.

People flocked to Jesus not just because of his teaching and healing. He accepted people as they were and was generous with his time and help. He was light, salt, and all the things he urges us to be, and people loved him for it. Are people drawn to us and to our churches today by those same characteristics?

Expanded translation

> It is best not to spend your time making judgments about others—you just might find them and God making judgments about you. For you will tend to be judged by the same criteria you use to judge others [if you are critical, people will be critical of you; if you are kind, they are more likely to be kind to you]. And you will receive in the same way you give [if you are generous to others, they will be generous to you, but if you are stingy, don't expect much in your time of need].

τί δὲ βλέπεις τὸ κάρφος τὸ ἐν τῷ ὀφθαλμῷ
τοῦ ἀδελφοῦ σου τὴν δὲ ἐν τῷ σῷ ὀφθαλμῷ
δοκὸν οὐ κατανοεῖς
ἢ πῶς ἐρεῖς τῷ ἀδελφῷ σου
ἄφες ἐκβάλω τὸ κάρφος ἐκ τοῦ ὀφθαλμοῦ σου
καὶ ἰδοὺ ἡ δοκὸς ἐν τῷ ὀφθαλμῷ σοῦ
ὑποκριτά ἔκβαλε πρῶτον ἐκ
τοῦ ὀφθαλμοῦ σοῦ τὴν δοκόν καὶ τότε
διαβλέψεις ἐκβαλεῖν τὸ κάρφος
ἐκ τοῦ ὀφθαλμοῦ τοῦ ἀδελφοῦ σου

But why notice the speck in the eye
of your brother but in your own eye
the roof beam not observe?
How do you say to your brother,
"Allow [me] to remove the speck out of your eye"
and behold [you have] a roof beam in your eye.
Playactor, [Hypocrite] first remove from
your own eye the roof beam and then
you will see clearly to remove the speck
from the eye of your brother.

Matthew 7:3-5 · Of Sawdust and Roof Beams

The exaggerated situation in these three verses brings to mind an old movie, perhaps in the slightly askew world of someone like Charlie Chaplin. The portly, rich, snobbish woman has a speck of dust on her gorgeous evening gown. Charlie tries to wipe it off for her, but his hands are muddy and his every attempt makes the mess worse.

Or here comes Simeon with a piece of lumber in his eye; the beam is big enough to support the roof of his house. He walks happily on, and doesn't seem to notice the huge protuberance covering half his face. He meets Andrew, who is rubbing his eye because a speck of sawdust blew in. "Allow me to help," offers Simeon.

The situation is completely ludicrous. But it is psychology at its most insightful, for several reasons. First is the relationship between a beam and sawdust: Both are made from the same material, though one is much larger. In the same way, we often see faults in others without realizing that those same faults are our own—and perhaps, much worse in us. If I'm irritated because Joe has to have the last word or Mary always has a better story, it's likely I do the same and don't notice. For instance, I'm annoyed by those who must chime in with better stories of their own. It took me a long time to realize I did the same thing, but I justified it to myself by calling it "empathy for the situation" when I'd add something similar that had happened to me. I felt this showed I understood, but after realizing how much this trait bothers me in others, I'm trying to practice being sympathetic instead of talking about myself.

A second psychological principle is that human beings tend to assign different degrees of sin to various actions. In Western culture, we generally see outward sins as worthy of judgment—sexual immorality in particular. But we rarely mention inward sins such as pride, arrogance, greed (sometimes masquerading as thrift), and egotism. Another overlooked inward sin is thinking only my particular group matters to God—whether that group is my church, my denomination, my race, my country, my socioeconomic level, or those who view gender issues the same way I do. This is why the Beatitudes begin with the very qualities that should make it impossible to judge others—understanding my own beggarly condition before God, my sorrow over my condition, my own humility, and my own search for inward righteousness for myself and justice for all God's children. This doesn't mean we can't agree that certain things are wrong. However, we must remember that those doing these things are also children of God. To them, as well as to people of good faith who hold differing opinions than ours, we need to show respect and acceptance even when conscience calls us to condemn the actions.

Jesus concludes by talking to the hypocrites and the play-actors who judge others without being at all aware of their own biases. He speaks to those who seem to know all the rules of religion but who understand nothing of the love behind the rules.

I do graphic design work as a hobby, and I do it well enough to impress people who have never attempted it. I have done a lot of reading on the subject, and I know the rules of composition—how to use similarity and contrast, choose the right font, use repetition appropriately, and choose colors. When I pick up a book, read a flyer, or see an advertisement, I notice the design details and how they work or don't work before I get to the message of the piece. And yet, next to someone with real talent, I am barely an amateur. I know the rules, but I don't have the real talent or the inward gift of an artist.

Too many of us approach Christianity the same way. We keep the rules enough to be impressive to others, yet Christ's heart of love, respect, and acceptance is not in us. We can't see past our prejudices of what a "good" person does to be able to reach out in any helpful way to those in need. The good news is that, unlike artistic talent, love for God's children doesn't have to be born in us. We can ask God for it; we can ask God to remove that big old roof beam from our eye in order to let God's light into our souls. Then we can, in turn, shine out to the world.

Expanded translation

> But why do you notice the sawdust in your brother's eye, and not notice the beam of wood in your own eye? How do you have the chutzpah to say to your brother, "Allow me to remove the sawdust from your eye," when—if you take a good look—you have a beam of wood in your own! You playactors! First remove the beam of wood from your own eye. Then you will be able to open your eyes wide and see clearly enough to remove the sawdust from your brother's eye.

μὴ δῶτε τὸ ἅγιον τοῖς κυσίν
μηδὲ βάλητε τοὺς μαργαρίτας ὑμῶν
ἔμπροσθεν τῶν χοίρων
μήποτε καταπατήσουσιν αὐτοὺς
ἐν τοῖς ποσὶν αὐτῶν καὶ στραφέντες ῥήξωσιν ὑμᾶς

Do not offer the holy thing to the dogs,
nor toss your pearls
before the pigs,
lest they trample them
under their feet and turning tear you into pieces.

Matthew 7:6 · Dogs, Pigs, and Pearls

Matthew 7:6 provides another example of parallelism and is similar to turning the other cheek (Matthew 5:39)—a verse that seems simple and straightforward on the surface but hides a truer meaning underneath.

First, the dogs and pigs in the Palestine of that day were neither domesticated nor farm animals. They were wild and dangerous. A "dog" could also be a culturally impure person, and pigs were not kosher. Both terms were deeply insulting.

We move next to the words *holy* and *pearls*. That which is holy is pure and dedicated to God. It represents the spiritually precious. Pearls were highly prized, as witnessed in the word picture found in Matthew 13:45-46: A merchant who found a perfect pearl and gladly sold everything he owned to possess it. Pearls represent the materially precious, and in the story of the merchant, the kingdom of heaven.

In a literal sense, we don't give pearls to dogs and pigs because pearls are only valuable to humans. Animals have a totally different idea of what is precious; food and water mean more to them than the most expensive pearls or the holiest items we might own. If I thought I was about to be presented with the answer to some great sacred mystery and was handed a dog biscuit instead, my emotions would run the gamut from confusion to hurt to anger at being duped. In the same way, a dog promised a juicy steak bone would not appreciate being given a holy secret instead.

From earliest times, this verse has been read the obvious way. The church fathers believed it meant that they were not to offer the sacraments to the unbaptized. Most today would interpret it that we are not to speak of sacred things before those who are against the Christian faith. And yet to whom did Jesus first state openly that he was the Messiah? To a Samaritan woman of dubious reputation. He also talked to Zaccheus, a hated tax collector, and Zaccheus was changed by what he learned. The people listening to this sermon weren't the highly educated, righteous religious leaders. They were the common people, the laborers, the uneducated, the sick, the poor, and the marginalized of society.

When people are busy protecting their own position they often can't hear anything else. The Bible, acknowledging this, often says, "The person who has ears, let him hear." I can't hear correctly when I'm defending my ideas or when I'm busy trying to prove someone else wrong. I can't hear fairly when I'm so sure I'm right that there's no point in listening to anyone else. So many times when confronted by something new or different or challenging, people simply put their fingers in their ears and shout their position all the louder.

There's no point in talking to people in this condition even if you may be offering a new truth or different pearls of wisdom. We see this in American politics today: Both the conservative and liberal parties shout their own truths more and more stridently, and no one listens.

It was the religious leaders of Jesus' day who turned so savagely against Jesus. It was those who were so caught up in their stunted interpretations of God that they were unable and unwilling to accept truth when it contradicted that interpretation. It was people in power who didn't want the status quo disturbed. It was the people who believed only they had the right answers.

We can keep from acting like dogs and pigs ourselves through prayer coupled with the attitudes taught in the sermon. We can shut our mouths and listen to other points of view. We can look for common ground with our opponents and learn to see them as human beings with needs and legitimate concerns. Once our comrades feel heard, they may be able to listen better, and rather than simply making the sounds of squealing pigs and barking dogs, we may engage in helpful dialogue.

Expanded translation
>Don't offer that which is holy to the dogs nor scatter your pearls before the pigs lest they trample them with their feet, and turning around, tear you into pieces. There's no point in talking to people until they can listen.

17

GIVING AS GOD GIVES

αἰτεῖτε καὶ δοθήσεται ὑμῖν ζητεῖτε καὶ
εὑρήσετε κρούετε καὶ ἀνοιγήσεται ὑμῖν
πᾶς γὰρ ὁ αἰτῶν λαμβάνει καὶ
ὁ ζητῶν εὑρίσκει καὶ
τῷ κρούοντι ἀνοιγήσεται

Ask, and it shall be given to you. Seek and
you shall find. Knock and it shall be opened to you.
For all the ones asking receive and
the ones seeking find and
to the ones knocking it shall be opened.

Matthew 7:7-8 · Ask, Seek, Knock

In the first verse of Matthew 7 we were encouraged to set aside judgment. We have been admonished to see to our own faults before we try to help anybody else and we have been reminded that some people can't listen. In Matthew 6 we learned to trust God to meet our needs. We are now in the right frame of mind to truly understand what we do need.

Many of us remember a time in childhood when all we had to do to get what we wanted was ask Dad or Mom. If we asked for something we needed that wasn't too expensive we were seldom denied. I required allergy shots as a child. It wasn't easy for my family to afford that medical regimen, but my parents found the money because I needed the protection. God is even happier to give us what we need. The Greek word for "ask" can be translated "demand." We are encouraged to present our needs strongly and without apology to our heavenly Parent.

We are assured by Jesus in Matthew 6:8 that God already knows what we need, but the process of asking helps us clarify our requests. For instance, many things need to be fixed in my home and I could produce a list of 20 projects I can't afford to do at the moment. Yet if someone told me "I will fix one thing on your house. What would you like?" I could pick one instantly. In the same way, a handful of needs and desires stand out at the top of our prayer lists. They may be as varied as physical healing for a loved one, meeting some basic need of our own, prayers for wisdom, or help for a friend facing a difficult time. Whatever the burden we must listen to the cry of our heart and then present that need to God in faith.

Our next admonition is to seek. This word recalls a detective story, for *seek* can be translated "investigate and you will discover." Seek also applies to a treasure hunt or children looking for Easter eggs. Many youngsters dream of finding a real treasure map with pirate gold at the end. When I was a teenager we used to have scavenger hunts where we were given a list of items and we went door to door collecting those items from our neighbors. After a weekend home from college I returned to find my bed covered with every stuffed animal and doll in the dorm. My friends arranged this so I would get acquainted with everyone as I returned the little critters to their owners. Once we reach adulthood, other kinds of seeking can pique our interest. For me, discovering just the right word to make a sentence sing is worth more than any treasure map.

Seeking is a little different from asking. We can ask for something specific, but sometimes our needs are not well defined. We may seek to discover our calling. We may seek to decide if a certain person is the right spouse for us. We may seek to know which direction to take or how to help a loved one. When I knew it was time for me to leave Seattle, I thought of several places I could go. I did the usual things like make lists of pros and cons, but when I prayed about it, God said "Wait." The seeking and waiting were well worth it. I have grown here in ways I would not have grown anywhere else.

The third and last of Jesus' admonitions is to knock. Sometimes what we need to do or ask for is not clear even to us, and all we can do is knock on doors until one opens. When the way isn't clear and all choices seem equally good or equally bad, sometimes it's necessary to pick a direction and start walking, or as the verse says, pick a door and start knocking. If we are attentive to that still small voice of God in our heart we should soon be able to tell if we have picked the right path or door.

What do these three words—*ask*, *seek*, and *knock*—have in common? They all involve action on our part. There is a time to wait silently before God (as in my example of God first telling me to wait before I left Seattle), but there is also a time to ask, seek, and knock.

One encouraging thing about these verses is that the verbs suggest corporate action. We do not need to ask, seek, or knock alone. We can do them together. We needn't ask only for things that concern ourselves, but also for things that concern us as a family, as friends, as a church, as a community, as a nation, or as a world.

The other good news is found in verse 8 where God assures us that when we ask we will receive, when we seek we will find, and when we knock a door will open. We are not left alone and comfortless. We have a God who knows what we need and has promised to meet those needs.

Expanded translation

> When you ask for what you need, it shall be given to you. When you seek for that which is dear to your heart, you will find it. When you knock on a door, it will be opened up to you. For everyone who asks, receives, and everyone who seeks, finds, and to everyone who knocks [the door] will be opened.

ἢ τίς ἐστιν ἐξ ὑμῶν ἄνθρωπος
ὃν αἰτήσει ὁ υἱὸς αὐτοῦ ἄρτον
μὴ λίθον ἐπιδώσει αὐτῷ
ἢ καὶ ἰχθὺν αἰτήσει μὴ ὄφιν
ἐπιδώσει αὐτῷ
εἰ οὖν ὑμεῖς πονηροὶ ὄντες οἴδατε
δόματα ἀγαθὰ διδόναι τοῖς τέκνοις ὑμῶν
πόσῳ μᾶλλον ὁ πατὴρ ὑμῶν ὁ ἐν τοῖς οὐρανοῖς
δώσει ἀγαθὰ τοῖς αἰτοῦσιν αὐτόν

Or which is [there] from among you
[from] whom asks his son bread
a stone will offer to him?
And if a fish he asks not a serpent
will he offer to him.
If therefore you being base know how
good gifts to give to your children,
how much more will your heavenly Father
give good gifts to those asking him?

Matthew 7:9-11 · Giving Good Gifts

Jesus' listeners must have looked at him incredulously: If God always answers prayers, then why were the Romans still in charge of Israel? Hundreds if not thousands of prayers must have gone up every day about that very situation, and yet, as Christ spoke, God's chosen people were still in the hands of Gentiles.

Although I have seen many prayers answered in my life, others have gone unanswered. If prayer is always answered, why did my best friend die of cancer? Why do innocents suffer? Why does evil so often triumph?

I don't pretend to have the answers to these questions. It is one of the biggest paradoxes of the Bible that we are assured all prayers will be answered, and yet not all prayers are answered unless you count "No" as an answer.

At the same time, Jesus' example is of a loving parent. If a child asks his or her parent for something wholesome and needful, the parent isn't going to give the child an unwholesome thing instead. But turn that around a moment. Part of a parent's responsibility is to say no to the unwholesome. We teach our children not to run into the street, not to touch the hot stove, not to be selfish with toys, and not to hit siblings. Some of these rules may seem unnecessary to a child. "Why can't I touch those pretty flames?" "Why do I have to thank Aunt Mildred for the ugly sweater?" "Why do I have to take this yucky medicine?" Parents give and don't give and encourage and discourage out of a wider knowledge of how the world works.

As human parents understand the bigger picture in this world, so God understands infinitely more than we do about what we need to grow and develop into mature Christians and what we need to learn for our unknown future. Though all our prayers may not be answered—at least not in the way we expect—we can trust that our heavenly Parent will do the best for us.

Verse 9 asks, "Who would give a child a stone when he asks for bread?" During Jesus' time in the desert, which we read about in Matthew 4, Satan's first temptation was to suggest that Jesus turn stones into bread. Perhaps this memory lingered in Christ's mind as he spoke. Jesus calls himself the Bread of Life, and in the Lord's Prayer we are taught to ask for the bread we need each day. When Jesus later feeds the five thousand, he starts with an offered lunch of bread and fish, the simple staples of life.

That Jesus used the fish and snake imagery is also interesting; one of the earliest Christian symbols was a fish. The first letters of the words *Iésus Christos Theos Uios Sotér*—Jesus Christ, Son of God, Savior—make the word *ichthus*, that is, "fish" in Greek. Snakes have been a symbol of evil ever since Eve's confrontation with one in the Garden of Eden, described in Genesis 2. The snake that tempted Eve is generally considered Satan in disguise.

The last verse is often translated as "even though you are evil...." However, the Greek word does not necessarily mean active evil. Especially in earlier Greek, it means simply "base," or "of inferior quality." Here the verse contrasts human beings with God and likely means "you who are so inferior to the Creator and Ruler of the cosmos." We with our limited knowledge and imperfect love can still figure out what is good for our children. When they ask for something wholesome, we don't trick them with the useless or harmful.

In Matthew 6 Jesus talked about the God who takes care of all creation, the God who knows just what we need better than we know. If human children can trust their parents to do good for them, how much more should we be able to trust our heavenly Parent? We don't give holy secrets to dogs or pearls to pigs; we don't give stones or snakes to children expecting food. Just as children live on milk in the beginning of life and move to bread and fish later, so we trust our heavenly Parent to feed us what we need for each point in our spiritual journey.

Matthew 7 is about choice. We choose not to trick our children because we love them; we choose to trust in a God who loves us, even if sometimes we don't understand.

Expanded translation

> Or which of you whose son asks for bread will pass him a stone instead of food? Or if he asks for a fish, will pass over a snake? Even you [pl.] who are so far below God in your understanding and grace have figured out how to give your children the things wholesome and needful for them. How much more likely is it that your heavenly Parent will see that you get all the wholesome things you need? All you have to do is ask.

πάντα οὖν ὅσα ἐὰν θέλητε
ἵνα ποιῶσιν ὑμῖν οἱ ἄνθρωποι οὕτως
καὶ ὑμεῖς ποιεῖτε αὐτοῖς
οὗτος γάρ ἐστιν ὁ νόμος καὶ οἱ προφῆται

All things therefore whatsoever you wish
that to you should do people thus
also you do to them.
For this is the law and the prophets.

Matthew 7:12 · The Golden Rule

We now arrive at the most well-known verse of the sermon, usually called the Golden Rule. Even taken out of context this is a good rule to follow. If people treated others the way they themselves would like to be treated we could avoid much suffering.

Recently in the business realm, the Golden Rule has fallen into some disrepute. In a strange sort of logic, business gurus say, "Don't treat the customer the way you want to be treated. Treat the customer the way he or she wants to be treated." They seem to be under the mistaken impression that the verse says, "I value this, so I'm giving it to you whether you want it or not."

I like science fiction and fantasy, so when my sister recently gave me a set of magnets shaped like characters from *The Lord of the Rings*, I was pleased. However, if I in turn passed them on to my mother, she would wonder if I had lost my mind. Worse, if I were to send chocolate to my father, who has diabetes, it would not only be a poor choice of gift but a downright dangerous one. Since we have been leading up to this verse through pearls before pigs and the giving of good gifts to our children, we know that it means something a little different than giving other people presents we wish were ours.

Verse 12 means we must take the time to be thoughtful about what we pass on to others. For my friend who collects gorillas, I adopted a gorilla from the World Wildlife Fund in my friend's name. If my customer values efficiency, I get his order to him promptly. If she values service and relationships, I take time with her. I don't prepare a ham dinner for my Jewish or vegetarian friends.

Verse 12 also means I must watch my attitude and treat everyone with respect. I must treat neither the person who bags my groceries at the store nor the waitress or waiter at the restaurant like a slave. I must be patient with those who are handicapped mentally or physically. I must not push the elderly or the young out of my way. The Bible illustrates this attitude with the story of the Good Samaritan (Luke 10:30-37). A despised Samaritan, the spat-upon and hated of Jesus' society, was the only one to take pity on a Jewish man who was mugged. He picked up the man and arranged care for him despite the fact that the Jewish people were his enemy.

We can all agree that if we were robbed and beaten, we would want help. Yet respectable Jewish people, too busy or too important to get involved, walked right by the injured man. It was the Samaritan, who had been looked down on all his life, who understood the victim's need. In the same way, we must not allow ourselves to be so caught up in our own lives and business that we are unwilling to reach out and offer the help we would want for ourselves or for our family. Nor should we allow feeling awkward or nervous to stop us, even if the victim is someone who is different or considered an enemy.

Absorbing this rule into our own lives could make a real difference in how we deal with others. We can ask ourselves:

- Am I treating my coworker the way I hope to be treated?
- Am I treating her the way I hope a man treats my wife?
- Am I treating him the way I hope a woman treats my husband?
- Am I treating that child the way I hope someone is treating my son or daughter?
- Am I treating that older person the way I hope someone is treating my father or mother?

- Am I treating the woman on the bus as I hope someone is treating my sister?
- Am I speaking about that celebrity the way I hope someone speaks about my brother?

The answers center on respect. I might not approve of someone's lifestyle or choices, but I don't treat that person like dirt or gossip about his or her faults. I don't put down my boss or others above me to my peers. Particularly if I am in a position of authority, I am careful to show respect to those beneath me whether I am a parent, a teacher, a boss, a doctor, or a prison guard. I show respect for those who think differently than I do on political or social issues, respecting the person even as I disagree ideologically.

Truly practiced, the Golden Rule is countercultural. We usually think of those with money or those in charge as being able to do anything they please. Instead, Jesus admonishes us to treat everyone with the respect we want for ourselves and to take the time to understand the needs of others. By living this way, Jesus says, we are fulfilling what God requires of us in regards to our fellow human beings.

Expanded translation

> To simplify what I've been saying, here's a good rule to use: When dealing with anyone, think about how you would want that person to treat you and then treat him or her the same way. By doing this, you will be following God's way.

18

αβγδεζηθικλμνξοπρςστυφχψωαβγδεζηθικλμνξοπρςστυφχψωαβγδεζηθικλμνξοπρςστυφχψω

LIVING
ALERTLY

εἰσέλθατε διὰ τῆς στενῆς πύλης
ὅτι πλατεῖα ἡ πύλη καὶ εὐρύχωρος
ἡ ὁδὸς ἡ ἀπάγουσα εἰς τὴν ἀπώλειαν
καὶ πολλοί εἰσιν οἱ εἰσερχόμενοι δι' αὐτῆς
τί στενὴ ἡ πύλη καὶ
τεθλιμμένη ἡ ὁδὸς ἡ ἀπάγουσα
εἰς τὴν ζωήν καὶ ὀλίγοι εἰσὶν οἱ εὑρίσκοντες αὐτήν

Enter in through the narrow gate
because wide is the gate and broad
is the road which leads to destruction,
and many are the ones entering through it.
Because narrow is the gate and
narrowed is the way which leads
into life and few are the ones finding it.

Matthew 7:13-14 · Know Your Gates

Two roads diverged in a wood, and I—
I took the one less traveled by,
And that has made all the difference.

(Robert Frost, "The Road Not Taken")

When we take a long car trip we generally get on the superhighway and take it to our destination as the quickest, fastest, and easiest way to go. When we arrive for a special event at a place we don't know well, our best bet is to follow the crowd because they are likely headed to the same event. When we go hiking, we often look for the well-marked, well-maintained trail so we don't get lost. When we are looking to find our way, following the crowd makes a lot of sense.

In gaining time and safety, however, we know what we give up. When we drive the superhighway we miss the wonderful, quaint little towns along the way, each with its unique atmosphere. We miss beautiful scenery. We miss the little rivers and the surprises tucked around unexpected turns of the road. When I travel from Klamath Falls to Seattle, I love to take the train. The tracks run along Klamath Lake for miles, and later head up a mountain pass through trees that seem close enough to touch. I see scenery that motorists never see. Those driving south into California along Route 101 on the coast see much beautiful scenery, but they may never dream how close they are to Jedediah Smith Redwood State Park, where part of *Star Wars: Return of the Jedi* was filmed. Walking through the redwood trees there, ancient and silent and pathless, is a feeling that can't be described.

Of course, not all trips off the beaten path lead to beauty. I remember one excursion down a narrow, winding dirt road where the road suddenly ended. It took what seemed like hours to turn the car around inch by inch. When you head off into uncharted territory you leave security behind. You don't make good time. But the journey becomes at least as important as the destination, and sometimes more.

Imagine a beautiful city on a hill, though you cannot see the road leading up to it. A superhighway seems to go in that general direction through a big beautiful gate. The road is full of cars, speeding along with no worries. Off to the side where you hardly notice it sits a small gate that leads to a narrow, rising path. The gate is labeled "Route to the City." Because the path is too narrow for a car, its travelers come on foot, together. It is a harder path but the fellowship is good and the views are breathtaking. It's not all beauty, though. The road leads through dangerous places and places where people need help. It runs close to the superhighway where the climbers must deal with the taunts of the motorists and breathe exhaust. It is most definitely the path to be on, though, because the only place the superhighway goes is to the dump. People may believe they are on the outskirts of the city, but they are not.

And what is this small gate and narrow path Jesus talks about (Matthew 7:13-14)? It is the path he has laid out for us in this sermon. We walk through the gate of the Beatitudes onto the path to God's kingdom. This is not an easy road. Early on Jesus warned us about the persecution we would face if we followed his teachings. And what about the teachings themselves? Love your enemies. Trust God for your needs, rather than put your security in your possessions. Respect others as God's children. Don't judge. Be humble. Do your best to make peace. Seek righteousness for yourself and justice for the powerless and disenfranchised. This is not life on an easy, safe superhighway, nor is it a lifestyle many choose.

These are some hard words from Jesus, but he never tried to minimize the difficulty of walking this path. It was not an easy path for him; it led to the cross. But he did walk the path before us. In fact he said, "I am the way and the truth and the life. No one comes to the Father except through me" (John 14:6). He has promised to be there to help us as we also help each other.

Expanded translation

> Enter through the narrow gate because the superhighway you see heading through that big impressive entrance is the road to annihilation. Those rushing down that road and speeding through that gate are the ones blindly following the world's way, the easy way, and the path of least resistance, like a flock of sheep to the slaughter. Because the entrance is small, and the path leading to life is narrow and difficult, there are few who discover it.

προσέχετε ἀπὸ τῶν ψευδοπροφητῶν
οἵτινες ἔρχονται πρὸς ὑμᾶς ἐν ἐνδύμασιν προβάτων
ἔσωθεν δέ εἰσιν λύκοι ἅρπαγες
ἀπὸ τῶν καρπῶν αὐτῶν ἐπιγνώσεσθε αὐτούς
μήτι συλλέγουσιν ἀπὸ
ἀκανθῶν σταφυλὰς ἢ ἀπὸ τριβόλων σῦκα
οὕτως πᾶν δένδρον ἀγαθὸν καρποὺς
καλοὺς ποιεῖ τὸ δὲ σαπρὸν δένδρον
καρποὺς πονηροὺς ποιεῖ
οὐ δύναται δένδρον ἀγαθὸν
καρποὺς πονηροὺς ποιεῖν
οὐδὲ δένδρον σαπρὸν
καρποὺς καλοὺς ποιεῖν
πᾶν δένδρον μὴ ποιοῦν καρπὸν καλὸν
ἐκκόπτεται καὶ εἰς πῦρ βάλλεται
ἄρα γε ἀπὸ τῶν καρπῶν αὐτῶν ἐπιγνώσεσθε αὐτούς

Be alert for false prophets,
who come before you in the clothing of sheep
but inside are ravening wolves.
By their fruit you will know them.
Surely people do not pick from
a thorn plant grapes or from thistles figs.
Thus every healthy tree wholesome
fruit produces but the inferior tree
wizened fruit produces.
It is not possible a healthy tree
unwholesome fruit to produce.
Nor can an inferior tree
wholesome fruit produce.

> Every tree not producing wholesome fruit
> is chopped down and into the fire thrown.
> Thus by their fruit you know them.

Matthew 7:15-20 · Of Prophets, Trees, and Fruit

"False prophet" is not a phrase we use much today; we tend to think of prophets as those who tell us about the future. In the Bible a prophet is not so much a foreteller as a forth-teller. He or she speaks for God. God sent many prophets in Old Testament times. They had two major messages: first, those who turn their back on God's commands can expect punishment; second, people must return to a life of righteousness and social justice. Micah 6:8 clearly sums up: "He has showed you, O man, what is good. And what does the Lord require of you? To act justly and to love mercy and to walk humbly with your God."

The first important lesson to be drawn from Matthew 7:15-20 is that Jesus specifically warns about people who claim to speak for God. In his day, he was talking about the scribes, Pharisees, and other religious leaders. Today he might refer to preachers, teachers, evangelists, writers—anyone in authority who claims to be bringing God's word to us. People who interpret God's words and who claim to speak for God are not to be taken at face value. In fact, though the general word from Jesus is "Do not judge," these folks are an exception. We are told to judge those who claim to speak for God, not in the sense of being judgmental but in the sense of carefully evaluating their life and their message, just as we evaluate ourselves against God's word.

The value of these verses is evident in the world today. Too many who are supposed to be God's messengers are not living lives in accordance with either the Beatitudes or the fruits of the spirit, which are listed in Galatians 5:22-23: love, joy, peace, patience, kindness, goodness, faithfulness, gentleness, and self-control. We can all think of television evangelists, priests, ministers, and others who have strayed from the narrow path.

How do we keep from being deceived? We tend to judge people's righteousness, yet none but God can know the state of a person's heart. But Jesus implies that it isn't such a difficult task to figure out if a person's actions and attitudes are in sync with God's words. We don't look at a thorn tree and expect lovely bunches of grapes. Nor do we look for figs on thistles or bushels of sweet peaches on a diseased tree. In the same way, we don't expect a healthy green tree to produce wizened apples. A tree is true to its nature; so is a human being.

Like the tree examples, people may perpetrate two kinds of deceptions against kingdom citizens. They may deliberately set out to fool the faithful; these are the thorn and thistle plants, trying to convince us they are grape vines and fig trees. Some early evangelists fit this description, moving from town to town with their elaborate shows and faked healings. People may go into evangelism today because it can be a profitable way to make a living, especially on television. Politicians and others may deliberately manipulate Christian voters by using Christian catchphrases. The fruit of these folks is obvious. They are either creating profit or power for themselves by promising what they don't intend to deliver; or they are manipulating emotions, usually pointing out some group outside the church, in order to heighten fears and create a siege or victim mentality. They offer to save Christians from these frightening things in return for a vote. But Jesus doesn't teach fear. He teaches reaching out, seeing others as God's children, and loving those unlike us.

The second type of person, more analogous to the healthy/unhealthy trees, is convinced he or she speaks for God, but actually teaches a message other than that found in the Bible. This kind of person is far more dangerous because of his or her sincerity. The Pharisees fit this bill. They thought they were doing the right thing by keeping even the smallest law to the best of their ability, not realizing they were missing the greater commandments of humility and love. People like this have initiated many of what we might call the crimes of the church: The Crusades, the Inquisition, the witchcraft trials, and the slavery of Africans are all examples, and we continue to reap the consequences today.

While we find it easy to judge those with moral failings, we often feel we shouldn't judge these sincere people because they are, outwardly at least, moral and often vilify the very people we ourselves fear. Throughout history, they have frightened us with, "The _____ are going to draw your children away from the true faith and destroy your lifestyle!" Depending on the century or denomination, you can fill in the blank with *pagans, Jews, Muslims, Catholics, Protestants, secular humanists, Democrats, Republicans, Liberals, Conservatives, gays,* or any other category into which humans have grouped themselves.

So how do we who are so inadequate to judge, do so? We must look not at their hearts—for God is the only One who sees the true motive—nor simply listen to their words. Instead, we must ask ourselves whether these people match up with sermon/kingdom values. Are they displaying humility? Are they insisting on justice for both sides? Are they acting as peacemakers? Are they displaying love for enemies? Are they respecting others? Are they looking for reconciliation? Are they rejecting stereotypes? Are they helping the poor and powerless? Remember Jesus' messages of love. Perhaps the simplest question, then, is whether these people proclaim love or fear.

When John the Baptist was in prison he sent his disciples to ask whether Jesus was the Messiah (Matthew 11:2-5). Jesus didn't say yes or no and he didn't point John back to the dove or God's voice at his baptism. Instead he said, "Look around. See what's happening here. See that people are being healed, and the poor are hearing the good news." Jesus' attitudes and actions were John's answer. We, too, are called to look clearly and honestly at those who say they are speaking for God, lest we find ourselves on a path that does not lead to the city.

Likewise, we must measure our own words, actions, and hearts against sermon values. We want to be healthy trees, bearing large crops of peace, patience, and love. We don't want to realize we have become diseased trees or find we have traveled off the path that leads to the city of God. There are two ways for fruit trees to be useful—producing harvests of beautiful, nourishing fruit, or becoming firewood. I know which I want to be.

Expanded translation

Be alert for those who claim to speak for God but are really pushing their own agenda, and for anyone who "dresses up" like a Christian before he or she comes to you and wants to snatch away God's people to satisfy his or her own ego and lust for power. Look at the fruit of their life. By a careful consideration of words and deeds, you will be able to tell if they are really speaking for God. Do they demonstrate the values of the Beatitudes and the crop of the Spirit? People don't pick grapes from thorn bushes or figs from thistle plants. Or look at it another way. Every high-quality fruit tree produces beautiful and healthy fruit, and the inferior or diseased tree produces wizened and unwholesome fruit. It is not possible for a healthy tree to bear wizened and unwholesome fruit, or for a diseased tree to bear beautiful and wholesome fruit. There are two uses for a fruit tree: producing eye-pleasing, tasty fruit, or producing firewood. When someone gives you a piece of fruit you can deduce whether the tree it came from is healthy or unhealthy by the state of the fruit. It's the same way with people.

οὐ πᾶς ὁ λέγων μοι κύριε κύριε
εἰσελεύσεται εἰς τὴν βασιλείαν τῶν οὐρανῶν
ἀλλ' ὁ ποιῶν τὸ θέλημα
τοῦ πατρός μου τοῦ ἐν τοῖς οὐρανοῖς
πολλοὶ ἐροῦσίν μοι ἐν ἐκείνῃ τῇ ἡμέρᾳ
κύριε κύριε οὐ τῷ σῷ ὀνόματι ἐπροφητεύσαμεν
καὶ τῷ σῷ ὀνόματι δαιμόνια ἐξεβάλομεν
καὶ τῷ σῷ ὀνόματι δυνάμεις πολλὰς ἐποιήσαμεν
καὶ τότε ὁμολογήσω
αὐτοῖς ὅτι οὐδέποτε ἔγνων ὑμᾶς
ἀποχωρεῖτε ἀπ' ἐμοῦ οἱ ἐργαζόμενοι τὴν ἀνομίαν

Not all those calling to me, "Lord, Lord!"
shall enter into the kingdom of heaven
but only those doing the will
of my Father in heaven.
Many will declaim to me in that day,
"Lord, Lord, did we not in your name prophesy,
and in your name demons cast out,
and in your name many miracles do?"
And then I will proclaim publicly,
"I never knew you.
Depart from me those working lawlessness
[that is, not obeying Jesus' words]."

Matthew 7:21-23 · Is Your Name on the Roll?

When the trumpet of the Lord shall sound, and time shall be no more,
And the morning breaks, eternal, bright and fair;
When the saved of earth shall gather over on the other shore,
And the roll is called up yonder, I'll be there.

(James M. Black, "When the Roll is Called up Yonder")

LIVING ALERTLY

These are the most frightening verses of the sermon. In no way do we want to reach heaven and have Jesus say, "Who are you? I don't know you. Go away."

These folks facing Jesus are not those who have tried hard to live honestly by kingdom values. These verses are not teaching us that we can't know until we get to heaven whether or not we will be asked to stay. The best news of Christianity is that we get in because of Christ's merits, not our own. If we have accepted that gift from him we are kingdom citizens. That's certain.

The people facing Jesus here are the same ones we saw in the last verses, so certain of their own worth that they never doubt they will be welcomed into God's kingdom with open arms. Look at their list of accomplishments. Didn't they preach amazing sermons and perform other glorious, important, and public works all in God's name? Yet these people were so busy accomplishing their own agenda that they had no time for the lifestyle to which Jesus calls us. These are the people who invoke God's name to accomplish their own goals, often for their own glory, and the people who forget the first attitude of the kingdom is humility. The Pharisees and the religious leaders fit the bill in Jesus' time. Likely we can each picture those who fit that definition today.

Jesus describes a time when people are gathered before him in heaven. Some stand awed and entranced by this amazing, unbelievable place. Some stand abashed, wondering if they should slink away from a location so grand. Others seem surprised to be there at all. Some stare at Jesus as if they can't get enough of that face. Everyone is here—kings and peasants, young and old, rich and poor, black and white, genius and mentally challenged, male and female, from East and West—a huge multiracial, multinational, multitemporal crowd. In the midst of all this comes bustling a group who look like they know very well they have every right to be there. Many in the crowd recognize them, and nod, remembering the great things they accomplished on earth. They stop before Jesus and the spokesman declaims in a loud voice, "We're here! What a pleasure to finally meet you after all the wonderful things we have done in your name!"

In a quieter voice, but one that carries just as far, Jesus asks, "Who are you?"

"Who are we?" the spokesman huffs back, frowning. "Look at your list. We are the most important people here—see all we have accomplished!"

"You names are not on the list."

"There must be some mistake! Let me talk to the management."

"I am the management," Jesus replies. "You served yourselves and your own glory all your lives, with never a thought to what I wanted you to do. Your names are not on the list of citizens. I don't know you. Go away."

As humans we tend to be impressed by competence and success. We are impressed by the rich and the powerful. We sigh when someone gives millions for a good cause and we are only able to give a few dollars. Even Christian organizations fall into this trap, making a big fuss over those who give large donations and ignoring the hundreds who give smaller amounts. Sometimes we attach ourselves to the powerful, who we believe can help to further our agenda, while ignoring our poor brothers and sisters. We glorify high-profile converts, and ignore the hurting in our own congregations.

Jesus gives us another way to live. We must treat people equally, regardless of their stature. We must be humble, merciful, and work for reconciliation in both small, individual ways, or, if called, in big, worldwide ways. We must show respect to all, even to those who would name themselves enemies. We must work for justice. In short, we must live as citizens of the kingdom in this world.

Expanded translation

Saying the right thing isn't enough to get you into the kingdom. You can speak in all the "Christian language" you want, but that doesn't guarantee you entrance. It is not the people who sound most spiritual who get past the door but the ones carrying out the wishes of their heavenly Parent as I've laid out those wishes in this sermon. On God's final judgment day, many will march up and declaim to me, "Lord, Lord, unlike the other poor wretches here didn't we give the people a message directly from you? Didn't we expel evil spirits in your name, and perform mighty miracles in your name?" And at that time, I will look at them and speak bluntly before everyone, "I don't acknowledge you or your works. Go away—you were always working on your own agenda, not mine, in order to look good in the eyes of others."

19

A FINAL STORY & THE REACTION OF THE CROWD

πᾶς οὖν ὅστις ἀκούει
μου τοὺς λόγους τούτους καὶ ποιεῖ αὐτοὺς
ὁμοιωθήσεται ἀνδρὶ φρονίμῳ
ὅστις ᾠκοδόμησεν αὐτοῦ τὴν οἰκίαν
ἐπὶ τὴν πέτραν καὶ κατέβη ἡ βροχὴ
καὶ ἦλθον οἱ ποταμοὶ
καὶ ἔπνευσαν οἱ ἄνεμοι καὶ
προσέπεσαν τῇ οἰκίᾳ ἐκείνῃ καὶ οὐκ ἔπεσεν
τεθεμελίωτο γὰρ ἐπὶ τὴν πέτραν
καὶ πᾶς ὁ ἀκούων μου τοὺς λόγους τούτους
καὶ μὴ ποιῶν αὐτοὺς
ὁμοιωθήσεται ἀνδρὶ μωρῷ
ὅστις ᾠκοδόμησεν αὐτοῦ τὴν οἰκίαν ἐπὶ τὴν ἄμμον
καὶ κατέβη ἡ βροχὴ
καὶ ἦλθον οἱ ποταμοὶ
καὶ ἔπνευσαν οἱ ἄνεμοι
καὶ προσέκοψαν τῇ οἰκίᾳ ἐκείνῃ
καὶ ἔπεσεν καὶ ἦν ἡ πτῶσις αὐτῆς μεγάλη

> Therefore, everyone who hears
> these words of mine and does them
> will be compared to a prudent man
> who constructed his house
> upon the rock. And down poured the rain
> and came the river
> and blew the winds and
> struck against that house and it did not fall,
> for its foundation was laid upon the rock.
> And everyone hearing these words of mine
> and not doing them
> shall be compared to a foolish man,
> who constructed his house upon the sand.
> And down poured the rain
> and came the river
> and blew the winds
> and fell against that house
> and it fell, and the fall of it [was] great.

Matthew 7:24-27 · A Building Lesson from the Carpenter

> The wise man built his house upon the rock
> And the rains came tumbling down.
> The rains came down and the floods came up
> And the house on the rock stood firm.
>
> The foolish man built his house upon the sand
> And the house on the sand went SPLAT!
>
> (children's song, author unknown)

Jesus brings his teaching to a close, and wants people to understand he is in earnest. So, as he often does, he tells a story, this time drawing from his own experience as the son of a carpenter.

The word usually translated as "wise" doesn't mean a sage or someone with great knowledge. Instead, it refers to someone who understands his craft. A translation that better carries the meaning would be "sensible," "prudent," or "experienced." Notice, too, that the man in the story isn't necessarily a carpenter by trade. He is not building a house for a friend, building a synagogue, or working on the temple. He is building his own house as we build our own lives.

So this man, this prudent carpenter, takes a look around at the available land. His options are the cliffs above a canyon or a wadi. It would be much easier to build on the sandy bottom of the wadi, but he not only understands building, he understands the climate in which he lives. So, although it is harder, he builds his house in a place where it is sheltered from the wind and high above the canyon floor.

Meanwhile, there's another man building in the same area. The word translated ever so politely as "foolish" gives us our English word *moron*. This is a man looking for the easy way with no thought for the circumstances. So while his fellow-builder hauls materials up to the high, sheltered place, our ignorant carpenter throws up a quick dwelling down in the sand, and then settles back, content, and watches the other toil away.

But life isn't all sand and sunshine. One night there is a terrible storm—winds roar from all directions and the sky opens up. The winds attack the sensible man's house on the rock. Like the big bad wolf in the story *The Three Little Pigs*, the winds huff and puff, but the house, sheltered and well-built, stands firm. Through the wadi the wind stumbles over the foolish man's house and, along with a sudden flash flood, rips the house from its foundation and it collapses.

Though some see this as a metaphor for judgment day—since Jesus referred to heaven a verse earlier—it is the conclusion of the sermon and so most likely carries a more general meaning. We have all experienced storms that threatened to knock us from our foundations. A mother loses a child. We get the word that we or a loved one is terminally ill. We get fired from a job. A husband or wife asks for a divorce. A drunk driver loses control, and suddenly someone we care about is gone. There's a tornado, a blizzard, an earthquake, a volcano, or a hurricane. We are robbed or mugged—or worse. There are all sorts of storms in our lives, and inevitably they come to all of us sooner or later. The point isn't whether there is a storm—the point is where and how we lay the foundation of our life.

The only sensible way to live our life, Jesus says, is to listen to his words *and then do them*. It's no good to simply smile and say, "What a nice sermon," and then go back to our life. It's no good to agree that the principles of the sermon are all very nice but quite impractical. It's no good to dismiss this as too conservative, too liberal, or from too long ago to matter. It's no good to say, "It was all right for Grandma, but this is a different world." It's no good to say, "My life is too complicated right now; I'll try this after I retire." It's no good to say, "These are fine for Sunday, but the rest of the week I live in the real world." We must absorb these principles and live by them.

The sermon outlines a way of life that's God-approved—the way of life of a citizen of the kingdom of heaven. It is radical. It is countercultural. It is not 100 percent achievable even for the saints among us, but it sets the standard.

It is not easy. It was much easier to build that house on the sand than to laboriously drag materials up the cliff. It is easier to take the superhighway than the narrow path. At the same time, look at the results of the easy way: a destroyed house and a trip to the city dump. It is easier to go along with our culture, but we are called to a different way of life.

The one who made us says the sensible way to live is by obeying God's words. Jesus walked the path before us. God sent the Holy Spirit to help us. Christ is our guide. Will we follow Jesus through that narrow gate and up the rugged path to the city? Will we build our lives on the firm foundation of Jesus' love and teaching?

Expanded translation

Therefore, everyone who will heed what I've taught you today and put the teachings into practice will be compared to a sensible person who built his or her dwelling on solid rock, safe above the wadi, where the floodwaters could not touch it. A sudden squall blew up and sent a flash flood racing through the wadi and the winds roared up and attacked that house and it did not collapse, for it had been built on the rock. And all who hear what I've said but don't take it to heart nor put it into practice will be compared to a moron who built his or her dwelling on sandy soil, down in the wadi, where it is easier to build but placed in a very vulnerable position. A sudden squall came and sent a flash flood racing through the wadi, and the winds roared up and stumbled over the house, and it utterly collapsed.

καὶ ἐγένετο ὅτε ἐτέλεσεν ὁ Ἰησοῦς
τοὺς λόγους τούτους
ἐξεπλήσσοντο οἱ ὄχλοι
ἐπὶ τῇ διδαχῇ αὐτοῦ
ἦν γὰρ διδάσκων αὐτοὺς
ὡς ἐξουσίαν ἔχων
καὶ οὐχ ὡς οἱ γραμματεῖς αὐτῶν

And when Jesus
had finished these words
astounded was the crowd
because of his teaching
For he was teaching them
as one having authority
and not as their interpreters of the law.

Matthew 7:28-29 · Astonishment at the Unique Teaching

Since this sermon appears to be a careful compilation of Jesus' teachings put into a logical order, verses 28 and 29 convey a common reaction to Jesus' teaching and so have an important place at the conclusion of the sermon.

The word for "astonished" is a very strong word in Greek. Literally it means "to strike out of one's senses," so this is more than just surprise. People were amazed, overwhelmed, and astounded. This was teaching like none they had ever heard before.

In Jesus' day, most religious teaching was done by referring to some authoritative writing on the topic. Things are similar today as we consult commentaries and other scholarly books to help us determine the meaning of a passage. However, Jesus did not teach that way. Instead, he explained the true intent behind the Scriptures, laid out a new way of life based more on attitude than on rule keeping, turned commonly accepted beliefs on their heads, and then said, "The sensible person lives his or her life this way."

No wonder they were astonished. And after reading and understanding the sermon as it was meant, we, too, should be astonished. It is not only completely different from the culture around us, it is far more profound than I ever dreamed.

In my town there are yard signs saying, "We believe in the Ten Commandments." I would like to have one that says, "I believe in the Sermon on the Mount," or "I believe in the Beatitudes." Rules and doctrines have their place, but to live by the attitudes of the sermon is much more challenging. After all, "Do not murder" is easier to keep than "Love your enemies." One is outward and easily judged. One is inward and requires a change of heart. If Christians began to really live by the teachings of the sermon, we might see a revolution as profound as that started by Jesus' disciples after Pentecost.

Though Jesus' last story talked about the sensible man in the singular, most of the *you*s in the sermon are plural. This kingdom life is meant to be lived in community. For those of us in the West with our culture of rugged individualism, this may be hard to hear. We tend to lead isolated lives, coming together as a Christian community once a week. Yet it is when we pray and dream and uphold each other together that we are strong.

So let us begin to see the world and our fellow travelers through God's eyes. Let us absorb the attitudes of the Beatitudes. Let us enter through that narrow gate that leads to God's city. Let us shine as lamps on a lamp stand, and bring God's light to a darkened world. Let us love our enemies as well as our friends. Let us become part of this grand adventure called the kingdom of God as we follow Jesus Christ, our guide. "Dear friends, let us love one another, for love comes from God. Everyone who loves has been born of God and knows God" (1 John 4:7).

Amen, and amen.

Expanded translation

When Jesus had finished speaking, the crowds were left astonished and overwhelmed by his teaching. For he was giving them the ground rules for a successful life, as God counts success, as if he had the right to do so—not at all like their law scholars taught, getting all their interpretations from others.

Matthew 5—7

αβγδεζηθικλμνξοπρςστυφχψωαβγδεζηθικλμνξοπρςστυφχψωαβγδεζηθικλμνξοπρςστυφχψω

EXPANDED TRANSLATION

Chapter 5

Beatitudes

³ You are blessed when you realize you are no more than a beggar before God's door. The kingdom of heaven is made up of people just like you.

⁴ Blessed are you who are brokenhearted when you realize how far you are from what you should be spiritually. God is your advocate and will take care of you.

⁵ You are blessed when you come to understand your true worth—neither better than, nor less than anybody else. You have become one of the true inheritors of the promise of God to humanity, for by living this way, you show that you understand.

⁶ You are blessed when you are desperate to do right to others, to treat others fairly, and have a burning desire for justice, for you shall be satisfied in that desire.

⁷ You are blessed when you reach out to others in compassion, because in your turn you will receive compassion from others and from God when you are in need.

⁸ You are blessed when you view the world out of a heart like God's. You will begin to see God everywhere and in everyone you meet.

⁹ You are blessed when you work to bring true harmony and reconciliation, for then you are acting as what you are—a child of God.

¹⁰ You are blessed when you are being harassed because of your emphasis on internal righteousness and external justice. The kingdom of heaven is made up of people like you.

¹¹⁻¹² You are blessed whenever people mock, insult, revile, harass, and say nasty, untrue things about you because you are mine. Living as citizens of God's kingdom, you are an affront to their whole way of life. Rejoice—and I mean be absolutely thrilled—because heaven is more than worth it. And when you are persecuted you'll know you're on the right track, because that's exactly how people have always treated those who speak for God here on earth.

Salt and Light

¹³ You are the salt of the earth, but if the salt has lost the very characteristic that made it valuable, how shall it be turned back into salt? It is no longer serving any useful purpose and will be thrown out to be trampled into the ground by passersby. In the same way, if you aren't making people thirst for the living water, you are not serving your proper purpose and are useless to bring people to me.

¹⁴⁻¹⁶ You are carriers of my light to the world. A city placed on a hill cannot be kept secret. Nor do I, God, put the light of my Spirit within you secretly, but I put you where all can see the bright light in you, and, through you, catch a glimpse of me. Shine that light before others, making God attractive to all you meet by your grace-full lifestyle.

Jesus and the Law

17 Do not believe as others do that I was sent here by heaven for the purpose of annulling all the words of God you have received through the years. I am the one who gave you those messages. Now I am the completion of them. I am what those messages have always been about.

18 Believe this truth: I declare to you that until this universe comes to an end and disappears, not even one dot or a single stroke shall disappear from God's written communication to you. However, listen closely to what I am going to be telling you shortly. I will explain to you the way the law was intended to be understood from the beginning.

19 Consequently, anyone who deliberately breaks or twists one of the least of God's commands, especially if he teaches people to do the same, shall be called least in God's kingdom—because he is least. But whoever keeps God's commands and teaches others to do the same shall be called great in the kingdom of heaven.

20 Let me be more specific. I'm telling you that unless your righteousness—both your private worship of God and your reaching out to others in God's name—is much more sincere than the outward show of righteousness of the law experts and their followers, the Pharisees, you don't understand what it means to be a citizen of the kingdom of heaven. Now listen carefully, because I'm going to give you some examples of what I mean.

Anger and Murder

21-22 You have been taught that it was said by your ancestors, "You shall not commit murder," and if anyone does commit a murder he shall be answerable to the law court and to human justice. I now proclaim to you that anyone who is furious with a fellow human being is answerable to the lower courts, and whoever deliberately destroys the self-esteem of another is answerable to the Supreme Court, and anyone who calls others uncomplimentary names shall be answerable for it at the final judgment.

23-24 If you are heading off to church to worship and on the way remember that a friend holds something against you, turn around and go make things right with that person first. Then you can come back and worship with a clear heart.

25-26 When you meet someone who is ill disposed toward you, grab the initiative and take the chance to make things right. If you don't, this person will continue making things worse and you could find yourself being hauled into court (literally or figuratively), condemned and sentenced before you know it. Suddenly you're locked up or locked out. I'm telling you straight, you will never escape until you have paid the fine determined by the court to the very last cent.

Adultery

27-28 You have heard that it was said: "Do not commit adultery." But I tell you that anyone who spends time gazing at another with sex in mind has already committed adultery in his or her heart and mind. Don't let your imagination and desires lead you into sin.

29-30 But if your right eye is constantly causing you to mess up morally, tear it out and throw it away from you. For it's a whole lot better in the long run that you lose one part of your body rather than that your entire body should be tossed onto the waste dump, where God doesn't go. And if your right hand is constantly causing you to mess up morally, chop it off and throw it away from you. For it's a whole lot better in the long run that you lose one part of your body rather than that your entire body should end up on the waste dump, where God doesn't go.

³¹⁻³² And it was said that anyone who divorces his wife must give her a certificate of divorce. But I am telling you that anyone who dismisses his wife for any reason other than unfaithfulness makes her look like she has committed adultery. And anyone who marries such a woman makes himself look like he is committing adultery. So stop and think how your actions affect others; have respect for your partner and for the promise you made him or her.

Oaths

³³⁻³⁴ᵃ Furthermore, you have been taught that it was said by your ancestors, "Do not make a promise you don't intend to keep, but fulfill all your solemn vows." But I'm telling you, don't swear at all,

³⁴ᵇ⁻³⁷ not by the universe because it is the throne of God, nor by the ground because it is the stool for God's feet, nor by Jerusalem because it is the city of the great king. Do not swear on your head, either, because you do not have the power in yourself to change even one hair from white to black or back again. If you mean yes, simply say yes, and if you mean no, just say no, for the extra words you add come out of the unregenerate part of your nature—that part that would let you weasel out of a promise.

Evil and Persecution

³⁸ You have been taught that it was said by those who lived long ago, "An eye to replace an eye, a tooth to replace a tooth, no more."

³⁹ But I'm telling you, don't oppose an evil person using the same tactics, but if anybody backhands you, turn so the other cheek is facing. That way, he or she will have to use a fist to hit you again, as an equal.

⁴⁰ And for the one wanting to prosecute you to the full extent of the law, even to taking the shirt off your back, expose him and

the law for what it is by dropping your coat, too, and leaving it behind you lying on the floor.

⁴¹ And if anyone will press you into service to carry his pack one mile, go with him two miles. That will take him by surprise, and may make him think!

⁴² Give to anyone who makes a legitimate request of you, and do not reject the one wishing to borrow from you.

Enemies

⁴³ You have heard that it was said you shall give honor to your neighbor and shun the one dishonoring you.

⁴⁴ But I'm telling you, love and honor your enemies and those who dishonor you, and pray on behalf of those who harass you,

⁴⁵ in order that you will turn out to be [genuine] children of your heavenly Parent; because God causes God's sun to rise on the wicked and the good and sends rain upon both those who practice justice toward others and those who are unjust in their dealings.

⁴⁶⁻⁴⁷ For if you are nice only to the people who are nice to you, do you expect a reward? Even the rich, who will cheat practically anyone, do that much. And if you welcome only your friends or those of your own social class, what have you done that's so remarkable? Even those you consider outside God's love and provision do exactly the same thing.

⁴⁸ Grow up! Start acting the part of mature adults. As your heavenly Parent is grace-full and generous toward all those who dwell on earth, so you should follow God's example and act with grace and generosity toward your fellow human beings.

Chapter 6

Don't Try to Impress Others

¹ But be careful! Don't adopt the kingdom lifestyle for the express purpose of impressing people; if you do, you do not have any reward from your heavenly Parent.

² When you do something for somebody because they need it, don't make a dramatic production out of it, choose rush hour for your "kindnesses," or play to the admiring crowd as some do. I can assure you their invoice is already marked "paid in full" and there is nothing else due them.

³⁻⁴ When you are helping someone in need, do it secretly and quietly so that your left hand hardly realizes what your right hand is doing. Your heavenly Parent, who also works behind the scenes, sees what you are doing and will take care of your reimbursement.

⁵⁻⁶ When you worship, don't put on a show for the crowd as the playactors do. Believe me when I say their account has been marked "paid in full." But whenever you pray, enter into your inner room (which is private and cannot be seen from the street), and having barred your door, pray to your heavenly Parent in the secret place. And your Parent, who likewise works in secret, will reward you.

Prayer

⁷⁻⁸ When you pray, don't think you need to build up a whole ritual and mysterious way to contact God like the foreigners do, for they believe their gods will only answer if they make lots of noise. Don't make yourself like them, for your [pl.] Parent, who understands you better than you understand yourself, knows what you [sing.] need before you begin your prayers.

⁹⁻¹³ Without further ado, pray like this:

> Our heavenly Parent, may you be reverenced because of who you are.
>
> May your kingdom come into being through us, as citizens of the kingdom.
>
> May your will be carried out by human beings as it is all over the created universe.
>
> Give us what we need for today, both physically and spiritually.
>
> Don't hold us accountable for our moral lapses, even as we also don't hold others accountable when they don't treat us as they should.
>
> Don't bring us into a place where we are tempted to do wrong, but protect us from the one intending evil.

Forgiveness

¹⁴⁻¹⁵ If you don't keep accounts concerning those who have hurt you, your heavenly Parent will also wipe the slate clean for you. Until you wipe the slate clean concerning what others have done to you, you won't be able to see your own failures and turn to your heavenly Parent for pardon.

Fasting

¹⁶⁻¹⁸ And whenever you fast, do not look excessively depressed as the playactors do; for they love to don the tragedy mask (hiding their true self), playing to the admiring crowd. Truly, I tell you, their account has been marked "paid in full." But whenever you fast, get ready for the day just like normal, washing your face and combing your hair, so nobody has a clue you are fasting except your hidden heavenly Parent. And your Parent, who likewise works behind the scenes, will see to your reward.

Security

¹⁹⁻²¹ Your most precious possession, whether that's clothing, money, stocks, or security, should not be anything able to be stored up on earth where it is vulnerable to decay, acts of nature, and theft. Rather, your most precious possessions should be stored up in heaven where they are not vulnerable to decay, acts of nature, and theft. What's most precious to you is what you are going to be thinking about and working for most often, so make sure it is something worth thinking about and working for—full of kingdom values.

Seeing Clearly

²²⁻²³ You see everything through your eyes—they are like a lamp. If you are looking at the world as God looks at it, you are seeing properly, just like a properly trimmed wick creates a lamp that can light up the room. But if your eye is not working properly, that is, if you are not looking at the world as God does, all your body will be gloomy, because God is light. If you have accepted that gloom inside you as light you're in trouble because it won't occur to you to seek real light. You have doomed yourself to live in the half-light of half a life.

One Boss

²⁴ No one can do a good job working for two bosses. For either he will like one a lot better than the other (and so work harder and better for that one); or be devoted to the one, caring very much about him or her, and have contempt for the other, hardly caring to be in the same room with him or her. You cannot hold dual citizenship in the world and the kingdom of God—your trust will be in one or the other; it can't be in both.

Food and Clothing

²⁵⁻²⁷ Because [you have chosen the kingdom way], I am telling you, don't be unduly concerned about having enough to eat, or

EXPANDED TRANSLATION

about what you are going to wear. You'll agree it takes more than just food to keep body and soul together, won't you, and that there's more to your body than what you're wearing? Look overhead—see the wild birds wheeling above us? They don't [have to] plant crops, or harvest the grain, or store it up for the winter and [yet] your heavenly Parent provides all that they need. Think of the difference between birds and people—you are worth infinitely more, more than you can possibly realize at this moment. Which of you [gathered here] by undue concern is able to add a single hour to his lifespan?

28-30 And why are you unduly concerned about clothing? Look around you at the ground. Think about how the wildflowers grow. They don't [have to] wear themselves out working long, hard hours, nor do they spin [fibers into cloth]. And I am telling you, not even Solomon in all his magnificence clothed himself [as gloriously] as one of these [little wildflowers]. And if God clothes in this manner the grass of the field, which exists for such a short time before being used for fuel, how much more surely [will God clothe] you? Don't you understand, you who have so little trust in your heavenly Parent, that God will take care of you as well as God takes care of the birds and flowers?

31-32 In view of what I've just been saying about the wild birds and wildflowers you should have figured out by now that you don't have to be unduly concerned about your needs being met. You shouldn't be asking such questions as, "Where shall we find enough to eat?" or "Where are we going to get something to drink?" or "What in the world are we going to wear?" Those outside God's family think only of eating and drinking and the latest fashions. [Don't you worry about that sort of thing], for your heavenly Parent [already] knows all your needs.

33-34 But your first desire should be for God's kingdom to be established and God's idea of justice and righteousness to come about. Don't worry about basic needs—God will see that they are met. And don't waste your time worrying about what might happen tomorrow, for you can't really guess accurately what will take place in the future. You will find enough to handle dealing with what really occurs without borrowing trouble.

Chapter 7

Judging Others

¹⁻² It is best not to spend your time making judgments about others—you just might find them and God making judgments about you. For you will tend to be judged by the same criteria you use to judge others [If you are critical, people will be critical of you; if you are kind, they are more likely to be kind to you]. And you will receive in the same way you give [If you are generous to others, they will be generous to you, but if you are stingy, don't expect much in your time of need].

³⁻⁵ But why do you notice the sawdust in your brother's eye, and not notice the beam of wood in your own eye? How do you have the chutzpah to say to your brother, "Allow me to remove the sawdust from your eye," when—if you take a good look—you have a beam of wood in your own! You playactors! First remove the beam of wood from your own eye. Then you will be able to open your eyes wide and see clearly enough to remove the sawdust from your brother's eye.

Dogs and Pigs

⁶ Don't offer that which is holy to the dogs nor scatter your pearls before the pigs lest they trample them with their feet, and turning around, tear you into pieces. There's no point in talking to people until they can listen.

Asking and Receiving

⁷⁻⁸ When you ask for what you need, it shall be given to you. When you seek for that which is dear to your heart, you will

find it. When you knock on a door, it will be opened up to you. For everyone who asks, receives, and everyone who seeks, finds, and to everyone who knocks [the door] will be opened.

9-11 Or which of you whose son asks for bread will pass him a stone instead of food? Or if he asks for a fish, will pass over a snake? Even you [pl.] who are so far below God in your understanding and grace have figured out how to give your children the things wholesome and needful for them. How much more likely is it that your heavenly Parent will see that you get all the wholesome things you need? All you have to do is ask.

Golden Rule

12 To simplify what I've been saying, here's a good rule to use: When dealing with anyone, think about how you would want that person to treat you and then treat him or her the same way. By doing this, you will be following God's way.

Gates

13-14 Enter through the narrow gate because the superhighway you see heading through that big impressive entrance is the road to annihilation. Those rushing down that road and speeding through that gate are the ones blindly following the world's way, the easy way, and the path of least resistance, like a flock of sheep to the slaughter. Because the entrance is small, and the path leading to life is narrow and difficult, there are few who discover it.

Look at the Fruit

15-20 Be alert for those who claim to speak for God but are really pushing their own agenda, and for anyone who "dresses up" like a Christian before he or she comes to you and wants to snatch away God's people to satisfy his or her own ego and lust for power. Look at the fruit of their lives. By a careful consideration of words and deeds, you will be able to tell if they are really speaking for God. Do they demonstrate the values of the Beatitudes and the crop of the Spirit? People don't pick grapes from thorn bushes or figs from thistle plants. Or look at it another way. Every high-quality fruit tree produces beautiful and healthy fruit, and the inferior or diseased tree produces wizened and unwholesome fruit. It is not possible for a healthy tree to bear wizened and unwholesome fruit, or for a diseased tree to bear beautiful and wholesome fruit. There are two uses for a fruit tree: producing eye-pleasing, tasty fruit, or producing firewood. When someone gives you a piece of fruit you can deduce whether the tree it came from is healthy or unhealthy by the state of the fruit. It's the same way with people.

Living the Kingdom Life

21-23 Saying the right thing isn't enough to get you into the kingdom. You can speak in all the "Christian language" you want, but that doesn't guarantee you entrance. It is not the people who sound most spiritual who get past the door but the ones carrying out the wishes of their heavenly Parent as I've laid out those wishes in this sermon. On God's final judgment day, many will march up and declaim to me, "Lord, Lord, unlike the other poor wretches here didn't we give the people a message directly from you? Didn't we expel evil spirits in your name, and perform mighty miracles in your name?" And at that time, I will look at them and speak bluntly before everyone, "I don't acknowledge you or your works. Go away—you were always working on your own agenda, not mine, in order to look good in the eyes of others."

Sensible and Foolish House Builders

24-27 Therefore, everyone who will heed what I've taught you today and put the teachings into practice will be compared to a sensible person who built his or her dwelling on solid rock, safe above the wadi, where the floodwaters could not touch it. A sudden squall blew up and sent a flash flood racing through the wadi and the winds roared up and attacked that house and it did not collapse, for it had been built on the rock. And all who hear what I've said but don't take it to heart nor put it into practice will be compared to a moron who built his or her dwelling on sandy soil, down in the wadi, where it is easier to build but placed in a very vulnerable position. A sudden squall came and sent a flash flood racing through the wadi, and the winds roared up and stumbled over the house, and it utterly collapsed.

²⁸⁻²⁹ When Jesus had finished speaking, the crowds were left astonished and overwhelmed by his teaching. For he was giving them the ground rules for a successful life, as God counts success, as if he had the right to do so—not at all like their law scholars taught, getting all their interpretations from others.

NOTES

Chapter 2

1. Faith Marsalli, "Breakfast with Jesus" (sermon given at Klamath Falls Friends Church, April 4, 2004).
2. James C. Fernald, *Funk & Wagnall's Standard Handbook of Synonyms, Antonyms, and Prepositions* (New York: Funk & Wagnalls, 1947), 319.
3. Jim Rohn, *Jim Rohn's Weekly E-zine*, February 18, 2003.
4. Kahlil Gibran, *The Prophet* (New York: Alfred A. Knopf, 1923), "On Self-Knowledge," 55.
5. Robin Williams, *The Non-Designer's Design Book* (Berkely, CA: Peachpit Press, 1995), 13.

Chapter 3

1. Marva Dawn, *Keeping the Sabbath Wholly* (Grand Rapids, MI: Wm. B. Eerdmans, 1989), 137.
2. Philip Yancey, *Rumors of Another World* (Grand Rapids, MI: Zondervan, 2003), 217.
3. Richard Rohr, *Everything Belongs: The Gift of Contemplative Prayer* (New York: Crossroad General Interest, 2003), 156.

Chapter 4

1. David Bloch, "MrBloch Salt Archive," *http://salt.org.il/news_arch.htm* (April 5, 2007).
2. Tom Sine, *Mustard Seed Versus McWorld* (Grand Rapids, MI: Baker Books, 1999).

Chapter 5

1. Frederick William Danker, ed., *A Greek-English Lexicon of the New Testament and Other Early Christian Literature*, 3d ed. (Chicago, IL: University of Chicago Press, 2000), 828.
2. Robert A. Guelich, *The Sermon on the Mount* (Nashville, TN: W Publishing Group, 1991).
3. William Shakespeare, *The Tragedy of Macbeth*, act 5, scene 5, (New York: Washington Square Press, 1959).

Chapter 8

1. J.R.R. Tolkien, *The Two Towers* (New York: Houghton Mifflin, 1988), 289.
2. Carl Honoré, *In Praise of Slowness* (New York: HarperSanFrancisco, 2005), 49.

Chapter 9

1. J. Michael Straczynski, "Secrets of the Soul" *Babylon 5*, March 4, 1998, broadcast.
2. Walter Wink, *The Powers That Be* (New York: Galilee Trade, 1999). I am indebted to Walter Wink for the phrase "Jesus' Third Way," which I first met in *The Powers That Be*. This book has influenced many, including me.

Chapter 10

1. Carl Boberg, "How Great Thou Art," trans. Stuart K. Hine (Hollywood, CA: Manna Music, 1953).
2. Philip Yancey, *Rumors of Another World* (Grand Rapids, MI: Zondervan, 2003), chap. 209.
3. Joseph Jaworski, *Synchronicity: The Inner Path of Leadership*, (San Francisco, CA: Berrett-Koehler, 1998), 47.

Chapter 11

1. Lloyd C. Douglas, *Doctor Hudson's Secret Journal* (Markham, ON: Thomas Allen, Ltd., 1946).
2. Martin Luther King, Jr., "A Letter from Birmingham Jail," April 16, 1963. *Martin Luther King, Jr. Papers Project:* http://www.stanford.edu/group/King/popular_requests/frequentdocs/birmingham.pdf (April 5, 2007).

3. Jerome Coopersmith, *An American Christmas Carol* (New York: Smith-Hemion Productions, 1979).

Chapter 12

1. *Gilgamesh: A Verse Narrative,* trans. Herbert Mason (Boston: Houghton Mifflin, 1970), 90.
2. *Gilgamesh: A New English Version,* trans. Stephen Mitchell (New York: Free Press, 2006). There are many translations of this oldest poem. This is a good modern one.
3. Sir Frederic Kenyon, *Our Bible and the Ancient Manuscripts,* 4th ed. (London: Eyre & Spottiswoode, 1939).
4. C.S. Lewis, *The Great Divorce* (New York: Macmillan Publishing, 1946).

Chapter 14

1. Ron Sider, *The Scandal of the Evangelical Conscience* (Grand Rapids, MI: Baker Books, 2005), 21.
2. C.S. Lewis, *The Silver Chair* (New York: Macmillan, 1953), 159.

Chapter 15

1. Abraham Harold Maslow, *Motivation and Personality,* 3d ed. (New York: Harper Collins, 1987).
2. Marva Dawn, *Joy in Our Weakness* (Grand Rapids, MI: Wm. B. Eerdmans, 2002), p. 59.

FOR FURTHER READING

Beatitudes

Howell, James C. *The Beatitudes for Today.* Louisville, KY: Westminster John Knox Press, 2005.

> Howell considers each of the well-known phrases in the Beatitudes and creatively applies Jesus' teachings to our contemporary world and lives.

Kolbell, Erik. *What Jesus Meant: The Beatitudes and a Meaningful Life.* Louisville, KY: Westminster John Knox Press, 2003.

> Kolbell aims to restore the Jewish roots and subversive edge of these blessings uttered by Jesus.

Lee, Cameron. *Unexpected Blessing: Living the Countercultural Reality of the Beatitudes.* Downers Grove, IL: InterVarsity Press, 2004.

> Insights into what the blessing of God looks like and how to discover life as God meant it to be—marked by wholeness, transformation, and freedom.

Christian Community

Palmer, Parker J. *A Hidden Wholeness: The Journey Toward an Undivided Life.* San Francisco, CA: Jossey-Bass, 2004.

> Explains "circles of trust," in which we learn to listen to each other.

Sine, Tom. *Mustard Seed Versus McWorld.* Grand Rapids, MI: Baker Book House, 1999.

> Sine's final chapters, in particular, offer a closer look at what Christian community could be.

Christian Living

Foster, Richard. *Celebration of Discipline: The Path to Spiritual Growth.* 25th anniversary ed. New York: HarperSanFrancisco, 1998.

Foster divides his book into distinct sections: (1) inward disciplines—meditation, prayer, fasting, study; (2) outward disciplines—simplicity, solitude, submission, service; and (3) corporate disciplines—confession, worship, guidance, celebration.

Foster, Richard, and James Bryan Smith, eds. *Devotional Classics: Selected Readings for Individuals and Groups.* New York: HarperSanFrancisco, 1993.

Fifty-two readings from worthy devotional writers from medieval times to the present.

Manning, Brennan. *The Importance of Being Foolish: How to Think Like Jesus.* New York: HarperSanFrancisco, 2006.

A plea to live transparent, kingdom lives in the world.

Miller, Donald. *Blue Like Jazz: Nonreligious Thoughts on Christian Spirituality.* Nashville, TN: Nelson Books, 2003.

Through personal revelation and bold proclamation, Miller's memoir calls readers to be authentic in their relationships with God, others, and themselves.

Yancey, Philip. *The Jesus I Never Knew.* Grand Rapids, MI: Zondervan, 1995.

A fresh look at the person of Jesus.

Peacemaking

Harper, Gary. *The Joy of Conflict Resolution: Transforming Victims, Villains and Heroes in the Workplace and at Home.* Gabriola Island, BC: New Society, 2004.

How to take responsibility for our actions, and proactively solve interpersonal problems.

Kahane, Adam. *Solving Tough Problems: An Open Way of Talking, Listening, and Creating New Realities.* San Francisco, CA: Berrett-Koehler, 2004.

Learning to listen as a way to begin to understand others' viewpoints.

Niyonzima, David and Lon Fendall. *Unlocking Horns.* Newberg, OR: Barclay Press, 2001.
Forgiveness and reconciliation in Burundi.

Prayer

Foster, Richard. *Prayer: Finding the Heart's True Home.* New York: HarperSanFrancisco, 1992.
This Quaker author surveys 21 forms of prayer.

Lawrence, Brother. *The Practice of the Presence of God.* New Kensington, PA: Whitaker House, 1982. (Various other versions are available.)
The classic book on prayer by the medieval monk.

Rohr, Richard. *Everything Belongs: The Gift of Contemplative Prayer.* New York: Crossroad General Interest, 2003.
The balance of contemplation and action in our everyday lives.

Sermon on the Mount

Stott, John R.W. *The Message of the Sermon on the Mount: (Matthew 5-7 : Christian Counter-Culture).* Downers Grove, IL: InterVarsity Press, 1985.
A popular writer from a generation ago expounds the Sermon on the Mount and the countercultural lifestyle to which Jesus calls his followers.

Willard, Dallas. *The Divine Conspiracy: Rediscovering Our Hidden Life In God.* New York: HarperSanFrancisco, 1998.
Contains an excellent treatment of the Sermon on the Mount.

Wink, Walter. *The Powers That Be.* New York: Galilee Trade, 1999.
Wink not only addresses the Sermon on the Mount, but includes a wonderful section on creative nonviolence.

Social Justice

Sachs, Jeffrey D. *The End of Poverty: Economic Possibilities for Our Time.* New York: Penguin Press, 2005.
Not a Christian book, but a straightforward look at how we might end poverty.

Sider, Ronald J. *The Scandal of the Evangelical Conscience: Why are Christians Living Just Like the Rest of the World?* Grand Rapids, MI: Baker Books, 2005.

How to live with kingdom values, not the values of the world.

Simon, Arthur. *How Much is Enough? Hungering for God in an Affluent Culture.* Grand Rapids, MI: Baker Books, 2003.

Learning to appreciate what we have, while living simply so that others may live.

www.ingramcontent.com/pod-product-compliance
Lightning Source LLC
Chambersburg PA
CBHW060506090426
42735CB00011B/2125